Authority

Key Concepts in Political Theory

Charles Jones and Richard Vernon, *Patriotism*
Roger Griffin, *Fascism*
Peter J. Steinberger, *Political Judgment*
Fabian Wendt, *Authority*

Authority

Fabian Wendt

Polity

Copyright © Fabian Wendt 2018

The right of Fabian Wendt to be identified as Author of this Work has been asserted in accordance with the UK Copyright, Designs and Patents Act 1988.

First published in 2018 by Polity Press

Polity Press
65 Bridge Street
Cambridge CB2 1UR, UK

Polity Press
101 Station Landing
Suite 300
Medford, MA 02155, USA

All rights reserved. Except for the quotation of short passages for the purpose of criticism and review, no part of this publication may be reproduced, stored in a retrieval system or transmitted, in any form or by any means, electronic, mechanical, photocopying, recording or otherwise, without the prior permission of the publisher.

ISBN-13: 978-1-5095-1697-1
ISBN-13: 978-1-5095-1698-8 (pb)

A catalogue record for this book is available from the British Library.

Library of Congress Cataloging-in-Publication Data
Names: Wendt, Fabian, author.
Title: Authority / Fabian Wendt.
Description: Medford, MA : Polity Press, [2018] | Series: Key concepts in political theory | Includes bibliographical references and index.
Identifiers: LCCN 2017056826 (print) | LCCN 2018004823 (ebook) | ISBN 9781509517015 (Epub) | ISBN 9781509516971 (hardback) | ISBN 9781509516995
   (pbk.)
Subjects: LCSH: Authority--Social aspects. | Authority--Philosophy.
Classification: LCC HM1251 (ebook) | LCC HM1251 .W46 2018 (print) | DDC 303.3/6--dc23
LC record available at https://lccn.loc.gov/2017056826

Typeset in in 10.5 on 12 pt Sabon
by Fakenham Prepress Solutions, Fakenham, Norfolk NR21 8NN
Printed and bound in Great Britain by Clays Ltd, Elcograf S.p.A.

The publisher has used its best endeavors to ensure that the URLs for external websites referred to in this book are correct and active at the time of going to press. However, the publisher has no responsibility for the websites and can make no guarantee that a site will remain live or that the content is or will remain appropriate.

Every effort has been made to trace all copyright holders, but if any have been inadvertently overlooked the publisher will be pleased to include any necessary credits in any subsequent reprint or edition.

For further information on Polity, visit our website: politybooks.com

Contents

Acknowledgments		vi
1	Varieties of Authority	1
2	Consent and Authority	17
3	The Service Conception of Authority	37
4	Community and Authority	50
5	Natural Duties and Authority	67
6	Fair Cooperation and Authority	83
7	States without Authority	97
Bibliography		115
Index		125

Acknowledgments

Many people helped in the process of writing this book and I am deeply grateful for their support. John Horton, Laura Valentini, and an anonymous colleague read the manuscript for Polity Press and provided generous reports with helpful and detailed comments. Peter Dietsch was kind enough to organize a manuscript workshop at the Centre de recherche en éthique in Montreal in November 2017. At the workshop, I benefited from insightful commentaries by Arash Abizadeh, Étienne Brown, Peter Dietsch, Richard Healey, Angie Pepper, and Daniel Weinstock. Moreover, Vuko Andric, Emanuela Ceva, and Anita Wendt read (parts of) the manuscript and provided valuable feedback, and George Owers from Polity Press was a great and enthusiastic guide all along.

1
Varieties of Authority

Most people have mixed feelings about authority. On the one hand, submission to authorities seems to conflict with our freedom and autonomy, and we regard it as an important youthful instinct to challenge authorities and to sometimes rebel against them. On the other hand, we have great respect for many authorities and we see the usefulness of complying with authorities. An explanation for these mixed feelings is that there are different types of authority, and that only some authorities are legitimate. In this first chapter, I explain what different types of authority there are, and I set the stage for later chapters (which will mostly focus on political authority).

Theoretical and practical authorities

Some people are authorities because they are experts on something. For example, Carolyn Abbate and Roger Parker have written a book called *A History of Opera*, and so arguably they are authorities when it comes to opera. On opera-related questions, their judgment should count. When we would like to know something about opera, it is probably a good idea to consult them (or their book). Let us call such authorities *theoretical authorities*, because they know more than others in a certain field. *Practical authorities* are different. A police officer's authority is not based on any special knowledge or expertise. A police officer can tell you what to do because she has the *right* to tell you what to do, not because she has expertise. Parents are another example of practical authorities. They have the right to tell their kids what to do, but their authority is not based on any special knowledge or expertise.

So what do theoretical and practical authorities have in common? One might be tempted to say that both provide other people with *reasons*, the difference being that they provide different *kinds* of reasons (Raz 1985: 211). Theoretical authorities are in a position to provide *reasons for belief*, while practical authorities are in a position to provide *reasons for action*. But this is not so. When Carolyn Abbate and Roger Parker say something about Verdi operas, others have good reason to believe that they are right. But theoretical authorities often provide reasons for action as well. Take physicians, as a paradigmatic example. Of course your dentist knows more about teeth than you do, and so if you would like to better understand the physiology of teeth, it is certainly a good idea to ask your dentist. In that sense your dentist is a theoretical authority. But, of course, you usually do not go to a dentist to gain knowledge, but to let him control the health of your teeth. During that process, you do what the dentist says. When the dentist tells you to open your mouth wide, then you have good reason to do so, because you want him to have a look and see whether you have caries or periodontitis. When your dentist gives you advice on how to use dental floss, then you have good reason to follow his advice, because you care about your teeth. Thus your dentist is in a position to provide reasons for action *and* for belief. This holds for most theoretical authorities. If you are unsure what recording of Verdi's *Falstaff* you should purchase, you probably should follow the advice of Carolyn Abbate and Roger Parker. Experts on opera are in a position to provide reasons for action, too. Conversely, practical authorities provide not only reasons for action, but also reasons for belief; when they tell you what to do, then you have reason to believe that you ought to do it.

Moreover, providing others with reasons for belief or action is not sufficient for being an authority. We all provide reasons for belief and for action all the time. When I bring a surfboard to the beach, others have reason to believe that I will go surfing. And when I start surfing and drown, others have reason to save me (which is a reason for action). This does not make me an authority.

So what is the mark of authority? What do theoretical and practical authorities have in common? Authorities provide reasons for belief and action because they have a certain superior *standing*. Theoretical authorities have a superior standing because they are experts on something, because they know more in a certain field. Due to this superior standing, what they do or think is "authoritative," not on a par with what others do or think. In the case of practical authorities, the superior standing is constituted not by special knowledge, but by having certain *rights*. The police officer, for example, has the right to make us stop and show her our driver's license. This constitutes her "superior position," since normal people do not have the right to make other people show them their driving license. The notion of "superior standing" is deliberately vague, but I think it is important to an understanding of authority. Not all forms of superior standing constitute authority, though. Being rich or powerful is not a source of authority, for example. The reason is that these forms of "superiority" do not constitute superior "standing." The superiority of having more power or money than others gives one more opportunities, but no standing.

I mentioned state officials and parents as examples of practical (i.e. rights-based) authorities. In the case of parents, one may ask whether they are not better understood as theoretical authorities. Compared to their children, parents certainly have greater expertise in most areas. Yet this is arguably not the only reason why they have authority over their children and it is not what marks their specific parental authority. After all, *all* adults have more knowledge and practical skills than children, and yet it is only the kids' parents that have parental authority over them. Like police officers, parents have authority because they have certain rights over a certain class of subjects, namely their children. (Of course, they also have certain duties toward their children, but these duties do not constitute their authority.) In fact, the authority of the state and the authority of parents have sometimes been thought to be similar or even identical. Robert Filmer, a major English political theorist in the seventeenth century, argued that the authority of absolute monarchs is based on the parental authority Adam had over his children (1680). John Locke put great efforts into showing that Filmer's theory does not work because there are important differences between the authority of the state and the authority of parents (1689). In the present context, the important point simply is that both the authority of the state and the authority of parents are constituted by a special set of rights. This set of rights marks their superior position, not some superior knowledge. For that reason, they both represent forms of practical authority, not theoretical authority.

Besides parents and the state and its officials, there are other authorities that have certain rights that put them in a superior position over others, i.e. other practical authorities. Bosses are such authorities. Maybe some bosses are also theoretical authorities, but again this is not what marks their authority. What marks their authority is their right to give orders, to fire employees, etc. The same holds for religious authorities like the Pope or the Dalai Lama. Religious authorities are often conceived as theoretical authorities as well, but what makes them a religious authority (at least as I would like to understand the term here) is not their knowledge, but their rights vis-à-vis the relative religious community. They may put believers under certain obligations, excommunicate people, etc. Teachers are another example. Teachers should really be theoretical authorities, at least in relation to their students. If they are not, they will not be good teachers. But their theoretical authority is not what makes them teachers. The authority of teachers is constituted by the rights they have over their students. For example, they have the right to grade them, give them homework, etc.

De facto authorities and legitimate authorities

As we all know, there are charlatans among authorities. This is especially so in the case of theoretical authorities. Some merely pretend to have the expertise that makes them authorities. In that sense, they are not *really* authorities. Now of course it happens sometimes that people are unaware that these are charlatans and still treat them as authorities. In a different sense, then, they *are* authorities. They are treated as authorities, even though they do not have the superior standing that people believe them to have. Accordingly, we should distinguish between mere *de facto authorities* and *legitimate authorities*. De facto authorities are treated as authorities; people believe that they have a superior standing. Legitimate authorities, on the other hand, really have that superior standing. Successful charlatans are de facto authorities, but not legitimate authorities. Conversely, unfortunately some legitimate authorities may fail to be de facto authorities. Sometimes people do not get the respect and acknowledgment they deserve as authorities in their field. Think of philosophers or scientists who explore radically new and much better theories, but are not taken seriously by their colleagues. Even worse, they may be treated as heretics at their time. When we are lucky, authorities are both de facto and legitimate authorities. Authorities that are only de facto authorities are problematic because people take them to provide reasons for action or belief that they are not in a position to provide. Mere legitimate authorities are unfortunate because they provide reasons for action or belief, but people fail to appreciate it. In this book, my main focus will be on legitimate authority. When I say "authority," I will usually mean "legitimate authority" (unless the context suggests otherwise).

The distinction between de facto and legitimate authorities applies not only to theoretical authorities, but also to practical authorities. Here we might not speak of "charlatans," but still there could be persons who are treated as practical authorities without actually having the rights that are needed to really have that practical authority. Think of the tale of "The Emperor's New Clothes." The Emperor is treated is if he wore his beautiful new clothes, but in fact he is naked. Some think that this is similar with the authority of states. They are treated as if they had practical authority, but they do not have it.

It is sometimes said that an authority has to be a de facto authority before it can adequately be called a legitimate or illegitimate authority. Talk of being a legitimate or illegitimate authority presupposes that one *is* a (de facto) authority. And there is certainly some truth to this. Yet there are counterexamples. There can be excellent scientists who are dismissed by the scientific community; they could be described as legitimate authorities in their field who are not de facto authorities. The same holds for practical authorities. A government in exile no longer has de facto authority, but could still be considered to have legitimate authority.

Political authority

The rest of the book will mainly be devoted to the authority of the state, although I will talk about other types of authority as well. The state's authority can also be called *political authority*. It is a specific type of practical authority, besides parental authority, the authority of bosses, the authority of teachers, and the authority of religious leaders. As a type of practical authority, it is constituted by a special set of rights.

Note that governments and states are not the same thing. Governments are one institution within the institutional structure of the state. It might be possible to have an illegitimate government within a legitimate state, for example when it came to power by usurpation. I will mostly deal with the legitimate authority of states, not governments.

For a start, we should get a clear picture of the rights that states and their officials claim to have. The right of police officers to make citizens stop and show them their driver's license is only a derivative right (i.e. a right that is derived from more basic rights). On a more abstract level, states claim to have the right to *make laws*, first of all. Laws apply to a certain territory and to a certain group of subjects. Some laws apply to everyone who happens to be in the territory, including tourists, exchange students, and asylum seekers. The criminal law is a prominent example. Other laws only apply to the citizens of the state, no matter if they live in the state's territory or not. For example, states often allow their citizens to vote, even if they live in another country. What is important to bear in mind, though, is that states claim to have authority over *all* citizens and over *all* people in their territory. Political authority has a "holistic" nature, in that sense (Christiano 2004: 267–8). A state that merely has the right to enact laws with regard to some citizens, but not with regard to others, or with regard to some people in its territory, but not with regard to others, would not have political authority as we conceive it.

Second, states claim to have the right to coercively enforce these laws. This is what the police officer from our example does, and so her right is derived from this more abstract right to coercively enforce laws. Of course the right to coercively enforce laws can also be seen at work in the praxis of punishment, for example. It should be noted, though, that not all laws are coercive in this way. Laws regulating marriage, for example, or laws regulating parliamentary elections, are not coercive in the same way that the criminal law is. They simply enable people to get married or to vote. It is true that even these laws have a connection to state coercion, since being married opens the possibility of filing new types of lawsuits against one's spouse, and these lawsuits can result in judgments that are coercively enforced. This fact is emphasized by Hans Kelsen (1934), who treats a connection to coercion as the essence of the law. On the other hand, this connection to coercion does not seem to be the *point* of laws that regulate marriage or parliamentary elections, as H. L. A. Hart (1961) points out against Kelsen. Be that as it may; in any case, states claim the right to coercively enforce laws, even if coercion is not the point of all laws.

Third, states not only enact and coercively enforce laws, they also claim that no *other* institution may enact and enforce laws in the state's territory without the state's permission. States, in other words, claim a *monopoly on the use of force*. The state may put a murderer in jail, but you may not lock a murderer in your cellar. Max Weber saw this as the essence of the state (1921), and many have followed him on this point. To claim a monopoly on the use of force means to claim an *exclusive* right to enact and enforce laws. It should be noted, though, that of course states usually allow individual self-defense, and so sometimes citizens may indeed use force. But this does not contradict the state's claim to a monopoly on the use of force. The claim to a monopoly on the use of force is just the claim that no one may use force without the state's permission. The example of self-defense shows that states regularly give such permission for specific occasions or situations. On the other hand, a state that permitted everyone to use force whenever one sees fit would stop being a state. States claim a monopoly on the use of force *and uphold it* to a considerable degree.

To summarize, then, states claim and uphold the exclusive and holistic right to enact and enforce laws for their territory and their citizens. This complex right can be called the *right to rule*.

The right to rule

But talk of rights is ambiguous. We should further specify what kind of right the right to rule is. It is helpful to follow Wesley Newcomb Hohfeld's distinction between different kinds of rights (1913). There are claim-rights, liberty-rights, powers, and immunities.

Claim-rights correlate with duties. When a person has a claim-right to something, then others have a duty to respect it. For example, I have a claim-right that others do not fondle my nose (without my permission), and this claim-right implies that others have a duty not to fondle my nose (without my permission). In that sense, claim-rights correlate with other people's duties.

Liberty-rights – Hohfeld calls them "privileges" – are very different from claim-rights. When I have a liberty-right to do something, then this means that I do not have duties that would stand in the way of doing it. When I have the liberty-right to grow tomatoes in my garden, this means that I do not have any duties not to grow tomatoes in my garden. Nothing is said about *other* people's duties here.

Of course, often claim-rights and liberty-rights go hand in hand. In addition to my liberty-right to grow tomatoes in my garden, I might also have the claim-right that others do not interfere with my growing tomatoes in my garden. But there can be liberty-rights that are not accompanied by claim-rights. For example, I have the liberty-right to park my car at a particular public parking spot, while you also have a liberty-right to park your car at that very same public parking spot. None of us has a duty to grant precedence to the other, and accordingly none of us has a claim-right that the other one does not use the spot.

Powers are second-order rights. They mean the ability to alter one's own or other people's rights and duties. For example, I have the power to sell my home-grown tomatoes and thereby confer my rights in my tomatoes on the buyer. I give the buyer new claim-rights, liberty-rights, powers, etc. with regard to the tomatoes. Promising is another example where a power is at work. If I promise to take care of your tomatoes, I thereby incur a duty to take care of your tomatoes and I give you a claim-right that I take care of your tomatoes.

Immunities protect one's rights from being altered by someone else. Thus when I have an immunity with regard to my tomatoes, then this means that you lack the power to alter the rights I have with regard to my tomatoes. You cannot sell them for me, for example.

So what kind of right is the state's right to rule? It is a bundle of rights. Some ingredients of the bundle are rather uncontroversial, others are more controversial. What is uncontroversial is that a state with political authority has a liberty-right to enact and coercively enforce laws (in its territory and for its citizens). Yet traditionally, the core of the right to rule and hence of political authority was seen in the state's claim-right to be obeyed. Whether this right is really essential to the right to rule has become controversial, and so I will not presuppose that the right to rule includes this claim-right. I thus work with a moderate conception of the right to rule.

Yet what cannot be left out – and arguably forms the core of the right to rule – is the state's *power to impose duties* on citizens and on people in its territory (see Copp 1999: 18–21; Perry 2005: 273, 286; Applbaum 2010: 221–2; Enoch 2014: 300, 306; Schmelzle 2015: 60–5). This power seems essential to what states do: Enacting laws simply means putting citizens under a duty to respect these laws. (In Chapter 7, I will briefly discuss conceptions of legitimacy that attempt to do without the power to impose duties.) One may wonder whether it is conceivable that a state has the power to impose duties, but not a claim-right to be obeyed. It is: When a state imposes duties on citizens, these duties need not be owed to the state. They can be owed to other citizens.

Besides the liberty-right to enact and enforce laws and the power to thereby impose duties, there may well be other rights, like a claim-right against interference by other states and an immunity against the state's rights being expunged or changed by other states. But the core of the right to rule is the power to impose duties.

Three clarificatory notes

Before moving on, let me add three clarificatory notes. First of all, it is important to distinguish powers in the proper sense from what can be called "side-effect powers" (see Raz 1975: 98–104; Estlund 2008: 118–19, 142–4; Edmundson 2010: 181–3; 2011: 345; Enoch 2011: 4–6; 2014: 299; Essert 2015). For example, when I am drowning and cry for help, I can thereby put a passerby under a duty to help me. This is not a power in the proper sense, but a mere side-effect power. But it is not so easy to say what the difference between proper powers and side-effect powers really is.

David Estlund remarks that side-effect cases are cases where "a requirement or prohibition is the result of certain acts of mine but where they are no part of the point of the act" (2008: 143). It is not part of the point of my going swimming to put you under a duty to rescue me. But, on the other hand, maybe it *could* be the point of my going swimming (it may really be my intention to put you under a duty to rescue me). Even if it were the point of my going swimming, this would arguably not constitute a power in the sense we are after here.

So there must be something else that is distinctive about proper powers. Maybe it is one's ability to create *new* reasons for action "by mere say-so." In the drowning example, my drowning and crying merely *triggers* reasons that had been there independently of my action. Your moral duty to help others in emergency situations (when possible without unreasonable costs) is triggered by my drowning. In other words, in a side-effect case I do something that causally changes the world such that a reason that applies to you independently of my action becomes relevant. With proper powers, this is different. Here my action – usually my uttering of words – brings a new reason into existence, by mere say-so. If I promise to take care of your tomatoes, I thereby create a new reason for action, namely a moral reason for me to take care of your tomatoes. Now one might be tempted to think that this is not so different from side-effect cases. Why not say that by promising I merely trigger a reason that was there all along, namely the reason to keep my promises?

Here is the third and most promising candidate for distinguishing proper powers from side-effect powers: Only proper powers create "content-independent" reasons for action. The mere fact that I promised something gives a reason for action (namely to do the thing that is to be done if I am to keep the promise), no matter what the content of the promise was. Of course, there are things that I cannot promise; a promise to kill someone is not valid. But a valid promise creates a reason to do the thing that was promised, simply because it was promised, and in that sense it creates a reason for action independently of the content of the promise. Going swimming and drowning does *not* create content-independent reasons for action in that sense.

The state's power to impose duties is a proper power in that it is supposed to create content-independent reasons for action, just like promising. Enacting laws means imposing legal duties and thereby creating reasons for action independently of the law's content. As with promises, this does not imply that there are no moral limits on the kinds of duties the state can impose. Even states with political authority do not have the right to order a genocide. The power to impose duties is a power to create content-independent reasons for action within the range of morally permissible legislation.

The second clarificatory note is that the state's right to rule is a *moral* right. Trivially, states have the *legal* rights to do all the things they do. In particular, states have the legal power to impose legal duties on citizens and on everyone in their territories. The interesting question is whether states also have the moral right to do the things they do. If they do, then they have *legitimate authority*. In particular, it is interesting whether states also have the moral power to impose legal duties or, if you prefer, whether they have the moral liberty-right to exercise their legal power to impose legal duties on others. It should be mentioned that Hohfeld's classification of rights was meant for rights in legal talk, but one can use his distinctions for rights in the moral realm as well.

Third, a few words on the relation between political authority and what is often called "political obligation." Just as political authority is a moral notion, political obligation also is a moral notion. Political obligations refer to the moral duties or obligations citizens have by virtue of being members of their political community. Political obligations include the duty to obey the law, to pay taxes, to serve in the military, etc. Usually, political authority and political obligations have been regarded as very closely related, as two sides of the same coin. If political authority contains a claim-right to be obeyed, then citizens have political obligations insofar as they have a duty to obey that correlates with this claim-right. But, as I said, I work with a moderate account of political authority that does not include a claim-right to be obeyed. Yet there is still a close connection between political authority and political obligations on this account, since states with political authority are said to have the power to impose duties on citizens, including duties to pay taxes, to serve in the military, and to respect the law. Now these duties are *legal* duties, first of all. But if the state has the *moral* power to impose these duties, then arguably citizens also have *moral* duties to follow their legal duties. Nevertheless, it is important to see that not all political obligations need to be connected to political authority. Maybe some political obligations are simply owed to other citizens independently of whether the state has any moral powers to impose duties (see also Raz 2006: 1004).

Many of the theories discussed in this book have been advanced to justify political obligations as well as political authority. I will usually try to focus on political authority, but talking about political obligations as well will be unavoidable. Sometimes (in Chapters 5 and 6) I have to reconstruct the theories in two steps: In a first step, the theory tries to justify political obligations; in a second step, it tries to move on to political authority. Sometimes (in Chapters 2, 3, and 4) it is possible to more directly focus on political authority.

A final remark on the terminology of "duty" and "obligation": Many authors use the term "obligation" for obligations that are created by voluntary acts like promises, contracts, etc. They use the term "duties" for natural duties that we have independently of such voluntary acts, like the duty not to kill people or the duty not to lie. Although not much hinges on this, I will usually try to follow this convention. But sometimes one needs an expression that covers both duties and obligations in this narrower sense. An example is my reference to "political obligations" right here in the last two paragraphs. I take it as an open question whether political obligations are duties or obligations in the narrower sense. Another example was my earlier exposition of Hohfeld's typology of rights. Claim-rights, I said, correlate with duties. If we follow the narrower terminology, we should say that they correlate with duties *or obligations*.

Theories of political authority

Different theories of political authority provide different accounts of how and why (some) states have political authority. Political authority initially looks more problematic than other forms of authority. It does not seem problematic that some people are authorities when it comes to opera, for example. What looks problematic about political authority is that the state's superior standing is marked by a specific set of rights that normal people lack. This seems morally dubious because we tend to think that all sane adults have *equal* rights. No one naturally has a right that other persons lack, and certainly not the right to rule over others. There are no natural relations of authority and subordination among persons. How then could state officials have rights that normal people lack? Political authority is such a deep and pressing question because it appears to be a violation of the equality of persons.

As we have seen, political authority is not the only kind of practical authority. Parents, bosses, teachers, and religious leaders are other examples of rights-based authorities.

Indeed the justification of the authority of parents, bosses, teachers, and religious leaders is important, too, and I will occasionally talk about them in the upcoming chapters on theories of political authority. But political authority looks more problematic than the authority of parents, bosses, teachers, and religious leaders, since the authority of the latter is not a violation of equality in the same way that political authority is. Children are not equals and so parental authority and the authority of school teachers is not an authority among equals. The authority of bosses is based on voluntary contracts and therefore arguably not a violation of equality. Likewise, I can escape the authority of religious leaders if I want to, and I need not submit to any teachers when I am an adult person.

Now one could object that political authority does not bring any new inequality between persons since the state *is not a person*, even though we treat it as an agent. But, in reply, while it is true that states are merely an institutional structure, real persons have to fill certain roles within this structure. The state is not a computer or a robot; human beings are necessary to bring life to the state. In the end, it is indeed particular persons that have the rights that constitute the state's right to rule. One such person is the police officer. She has the right to stop drivers and make them show her their driver's license, and this is a right that normal persons lack. One cannot discuss the right to rule of the state without discussing the right to rule that persons have over other persons.

It is true, though, that the police officer has only a small share of the state's right to rule. The right to rule is dispersed over different roles within the institutional structure of the state and hence over different persons. Most importantly, one part of the institutional structure of a state will be the legislature, which has the right to enact laws and thereby impose duties on citizens. Members of the legislature (be it members of a parliament, be it an absolute monarch) thus command the most important part of the right to rule.

The task of a theory of political authority is to explain how and why states (and the particular persons who fill certain roles within the state) could have political authority. What makes a good and successful theory of political authority?

Obviously, it should actually explain how and why the state could have the right to rule. It is not enough to simply stipulate that it has political authority when certain conditions are met; we want a meaningful explanation, and one that is based on plausible and widely shared moral premises. It is also not enough to merely identify conditions that may sometimes be relevant to political authority, but sometimes not; what we want to know is what the necessary and sufficient conditions for political authority are. Let us call this the *explanation condition*.

If the theory can also account for other forms of authority, be it the authority of parents, bosses, teachers, religious leaders, or theoretical authorities, then this is certainly a great advantage. It gives the theory some unifying power. If the theory cannot account for other forms of authority, it should have an explanation of why these other forms of authority are too different to be accounted for. In other words, a theory should be able to specify its target and its limits. Let us call this the *target condition*.

A theory could be correct as an account of the conditions that would make a state have political authority, while as a matter of fact no states meet these conditions. If we have to conclude that all existing and very probably all future states actually lack political authority, then the theory is unsuccessful. Of course, this does not imply that the theory is false; but it means that the theory cannot show that any states have political authority. A successful theory, in contrast, allows at least some actual or feasible future states to actually have political authority. Let us call this the *success condition*.

In the following five chapters, I will discuss five prominent theories of political authority. I will refer back to the *explanation*, *target*, and *success conditions* and examine whether the theories meet them. Of course, my answers will only be tentative. This is a short book and I cannot claim to provide a final assessment of the prospects of the five theories. Yet I do think that I can show how hard it is for them to convincingly explain political authority. In fact, I am skeptical that any one of the five theories could succeed. In the last chapter, I will therefore discuss what we are to conclude if they all fail.

Summary

The superior standing of theoretical authorities is constituted by their knowledge; the superior standing of practical authorities is constituted by their rights. Mere de facto authorities are treated as if they had such superior standing; legitimate authorities actually have it. Political authority is the type of practical authority that states claim to have. It means the holistic and exclusive right to enact and enforce laws in a certain territory and for a set of citizens. To show that states actually have political authority, a theory must meet the *explanation*, *target*, and *success conditions*.

2
Consent and Authority

Consent theory takes states to have political authority if and only if they have the consent of the governed. It has a great history in Western philosophy: Thomas Hobbes, John Locke, and Jean-Jacques Rousseau all argued that the state is founded in an original contract among the governed and in that sense based on people's consent. The roots of this view go as far back as Plato's *Crito*.

Explicit consent

It is clear that consent matters morally. It can turn something morally impermissible into something morally permissible. For example, it is morally impermissible for me to bring some scissors to my next ride in a crowded subway and cut other people's hair when they do not notice. But if I am a hairdresser, then of course people can come to my barbershop and give me permission to do exactly that, when they consent to let me cut their hair. Their consent to have their hair cut by me turns a morally impermissible action into a morally permissible action. Similarly, one can consent to surgery, sex, and many other things, and thereby turn something impermissible into something permissible.

Consent can do this because it is the exercise of a

Hohfeldian power (see p. 9). It can create new liberty-rights. When a customer comes to my barbershop and consents to have her hair cut, she thereby gives me the moral liberty-right to cut her hair. But consent can also give rise to new duties, claim-rights, and powers. When a customer comes to my barbershop and consents to have her hair cut, she thereby also incurs a duty to pay me afterwards, and I get a claim-right to be paid. I also get the power to waive my claim-right to be paid.

In general, then, consent can explain how new rights can come into existence. That consent has this power is a widely accepted and commonsensical moral idea. Since explaining political authority means explaining how and why the state could have the *right* to rule, consent certainly is a highly promising candidate for explaining political authority. It can explain how the powers and liberty-rights that form the state's right to rule can come into being and thus meets the *explanation condition* (see p. 15).

In the first chapter, I said that political authority is particularly puzzling because it constitutes an inequality in rights. Consent theory could nicely explain and justify that inequality. Since consent can create new rights, it can obviously result in an unequal distribution of rights. If political authority is grounded in consent, then the inequality that comes with political authority no longer looks problematic.

In a way, consent theory tries to assimilate the authority of the state to the authority of bosses in the economic sphere. The authority of bosses initially looks less problematic than political authority because people voluntarily accept jobs and are free to leave their jobs. Their contract usually specifies that the boss has the rights to give (certain kinds of) orders. This does not mean that there are no moral requirements for the exercise of authority in firms (see McMahon 1994; Anderson 2017), but still the authority of bosses is consensual in an important sense. The authority of religious leaders and the authority of teachers who teach adult persons can arguably be explained as consensual as well. Consent theory tries to show that the authority of the state is based on consent, too.

It is clear that theoretical authorities – for example the authority of physicians – need not be based on consent, since their authority does not constitute any inequality of rights. So consent theory does not account for all kinds of authority, but it has a good explanation for that: It wants to explain the rise of new rights, and so it does not apply to theoretical authorities. But why should the authority of parents not be based on consent as well? As mentioned earlier, the assumed equality of rights holds among sane adults, not among all human beings including small children or human embryos. Small children and human embryos do not even have the power to give consent to the state's or their parents' authority. Human embryos and small children do not have the power to give or withhold consent to anything. Slightly older children have the power to give or withhold consent to little things they understand, like whether they would like to go to the zoo, whether they want to have some chocolate ice cream, etc. But they do not have the power to give or withhold consent to authority. For that reason, the authority of parents (and the authority of school teachers) cannot and need not be based on voluntary consent, even though it is a form of practical authority. Consent theory meets the *target condition*.

Do states have our explicit consent?

Now the question is whether consent theory can show that any real states actually *have* political authority. It is one thing to claim that states need the consent of the governed in order to have authority; it is quite another to show that any states actually received that consent. But before asking whether some states actually have authority based on consent, I would like to briefly discuss two fundamental objections to consent theory as applied to political authority.

One is that consent cannot be sufficient for political authority, because there are some things – namely grossly immoral things – that no government can require us to do, no matter if we consented to its authority or not (Buchanan 2002: 702). In reply, it is true that one has to invoke moral principles to determine the *limits* of legitimate authority. But this does not undermine the claim that consent is sufficient for political authority, whatever the limits of political authority are. Similarly, of course there are limits to what a surgeon may do to us, but this does not undermine the claim that consent to undergo surgery is sufficient for making this surgery permissible.

A second fundamental objection is that consent to the state must in the end be based on nonconsensual foundations: We need state institutions to determine what constitutes valid consent to the state, and we need state institutions to determine what precisely one consents to when consenting to the state (see Horton 1992: 42–3; Buchanan 2002: 700–2; Christiano 2004: 283–4). But a defender of consent theory can and should deny that one needs state institutions or any other nonconsensual authorities for expressing valid and determinate consent. Without such institutions, it may be harder to have precise rules for the practice of consent, but it is not impossible. Moreover, even if consent to the state did presuppose state institutions, this would not undermine consent theory. It would still make sense to claim that state institutions need our consent in order to have legitimate authority.

So let us get back to the question of whether any states have the consent of the governed. Locke thinks that some states do indeed have political authority. Let us take a quick look at his theory. Locke makes clear that – in contrast to the authority of parents – the authority of states can only be based on consent because adult persons are equals:

> Men being [...], by Nature, all free, equal and independent, no one can be put out of this Estate, and subjected to the Political Power of another, without his own *Consent*. The only way whereby any one devests himself of his Natural Liberty, and *puts on the bonds of Civil Society* is by agreeing with other Men to joyn and unite into a Community, for their comfortable, safe, and peaceable living one amongst another, in a secure Enjoyment of their Properties, and a greater Security against any that are not of it. (1689: §95)

He imagines a pre-political state of nature in which all persons are free and equal, albeit governed by a "law of nature" (which is given by God). This law of nature, among other things, grants people equal natural rights including the right to acquire private property (1689: §§25–7). Accordingly, it also gives everyone natural duties not to harm others in their life, liberty, or possessions (1689: §§6, 87). In the American Declaration of Independence, one of the most famous phrases sounds very Lockean: "We hold these truths to be self-evident, that all men are created equal, that they are endowed by their Creator with certain unalienable Rights, that among these are Life, Liberty and the pursuit of Happiness." The inequality in rights that comes with political society can thus only be vindicated by consent.

But do states have our consent? Locke seemed to assume that some states indeed were *founded* consensually, and he mentions Rome, Venice, and Peru as examples (1689: §§102–3). But, first of all, this is quite implausible (with some rare and small-scale exceptions like the Mayflower Compact from 1620). States are usually imposed on at least some non-consenting adults. Even the United States of America of course were not founded on actual consent. The Declaration of Independence was not signed by all residents, even though it declares that governments derive "their just powers from the consent of the governed." Of course the Declaration of Independence was signed by *delegates* of all colonies who claimed to represent their citizens. But not everyone consented to let the delegates speak for him or her. Moreover, slaves and Native Americans were not represented at all.

Second, and this is a problem Locke recognized as well (1689: §116), even if states were *founded* consensually, this consent could not bind later generations. Think of yourself: Did you ever give consent to the authority of the state you are living in? You did not. You were not even asked whether you would like to give consent or withhold consent. Consent theory might be the correct theory of political authority: It might specify the correct necessary and sufficient conditions for state authority (namely: everyone's consent is required). But if this is correct, we have to conclude that all actual states and very probably all future states *lack* political authority. In that sense it fails as a theory of political authority: It does not meet the *success condition*.

Tacit consent

But maybe the idea of *tacit consent* can help. The difference between explicit and tacit consent is not that one utters words in the former type of consent. One can give explicit consent by simply nodding one's head or raising one's hand. The difference between explicit and tacit consent is that in the former type of consent one performs an action whose only standard public purpose is to give consent (see also Simmons 1998: 166). When giving tacit consent, one gives consent without performing an action whose only standard public purpose is to give consent. In any case, both explicit and tacit consent *are* consent and as such they are morally transformative; they can create new rights.

But tacit consent is trickier, of course, because it seems unclear both under what conditions tacit consent is given and what exactly one consents *to* when tacit consent is given. Conventions are crucial here. For example, one gives tacit consent to pay the bill once one takes a seat and orders a meal in a restaurant. One need not explicitly say that one will later pay the bill.

There are some general rules that conventions about tacit consent ought to follow (and in fact tend to follow). First, John Simmons points out that "*all* consent [...] should be understood to be consent *to* all and only that which is necessary to the *purpose* for which the consent is given, unless other terms are *explicitly* stated" (1998: 167). In the restaurant example, the purpose is to get dinner in a smooth market transaction. That is why ordering a meal is taken as consent to do one's part in the transaction, i.e. pay the check, and nothing more. One does not thereby consent to return to the restaurant in the future, to support it with a donation, etc.

Second, another plausible general rule for conventions governing tacit consent is that they should track what people want. People should normally approve of the things they are taken to have consented to. This does not mean that one cannot give tacit consent when choosing among two evils. It is certainly possible to give valid consent in choice situations where one likes neither of the options. For example, I might dislike the only two hairdressers in town and dream of a better hairdresser, and yet I can give valid consent that allows one of them to cut my hair. Given the tragic situation, I want that hairdresser to cut my hair. Approval thus means something like "given the circumstances, the person really wants to give the consent he is taken to give." Conventions governing tacit consent should be approval-tracking in that sense. This does not mean that consent is invalid when a person gave consent to something she does not approve of. People sometimes act irrationally or suffer from weakness of will. The general rule should be understood as saying that insofar the conventions governing tacit consent *generally* fail to be approval-tracking, they should be rejected.

Third, another general rule for conventions governing tacit consent is that tacit consent can only be given by people who are in a clear choice situation. People should be aware that they can either give tacit consent or do something else to express dissent. They should be able to *control* whether they give consent or not. Conventions that do not allow the subjects to control whether they consent or not are dysfunctional, since consent is to be an expression of the will. It should be given knowingly and intentionally.

Fourth, conventions governing tacit consent should require that people are not coerced to refrain from expressing dissent. This does not mean that dissent cannot be costly. One may have to make a hard choice and in the end give valid consent to undergo some medical procedure, even though the costs are very painful side-effects. What the fourth rule is to rule out is that coerced consent counts as valid consent. To understand what coerced consent is, it might be worth taking a look at Hobbes's theory.

The state of nature as Hobbes describes it is quite different from Locke's. There are no natural rights to life, liberty, and property in the state of nature, merely one liberty-right, namely "the liberty each man hath, to use his own power, as he will himself, for the preservation of his own nature, that is to say, of his own life" (1651: Ch. 14). Hobbes also speaks of a "right to every thing, even to one another's body." Evidently, this liberty-right does not correlate with any duties. Under these conditions, it is rational for every individual to preventively attack others to preserve his own life and possessions, and so the state of nature becomes a state of war, according to Hobbes (1651: Ch. 13). To achieve peace, people create the state in an original contract in which they renounce their right to everything. In this covenant, it is "as if every man should say to every man, *I authorize and give up my right of governing myself, to this man, or to this assembly of men, on the condition, that thou give up thy right to him, and authorize all his actions in like manner*" (1651: Ch. 17).

Yet later in the book, Hobbes surprisingly argues that a state in which "the sovereign power is acquired by force" has exactly the same rights as a state "by institution" (1651: Ch. 20). Does that mean that the state's authority need *not* be based on consent after all? No, Hobbes seems to think that even conquerors who acquire their position by force have authority by consent. A sovereign by acquisition differs from a sovereign by institution "only in this, that men who choose their sovereign, do it for fear of one another, and not him whom they institute: but in this case, they subject themselves, to him they are afraid of. In both cases they do it for fear" (1651: Ch. 20). The problem with Hobbes's proposal is that consent is invalidated when it is coerced. Gregory Kavka helpfully distinguishes forced consent from coerced consent (1986: 396): You can indeed give valid consent when you are in unfortunate circumstances that force you to choose between two bad options and give consent to one of them. To claim otherwise would mean to disallow people to try to make the best of their situation. Forced consent, therefore, is valid. But things are different when the party you are dealing with has *put* you in the unfortunate circumstances *in order* to make you consent to something. Take the case of a saboteur who manipulates a woman's car in order to later be able to offer her to repair it if she sleeps with him (say in the desert, where nobody else is around). Here, it seems that the woman does not incur any obligations when she gives consent to his proposal and the saboteur does not receive a right to have sex with her. Coerced consent is invalid and does not give rise to new rights and obligations. For the same reason, Hobbesian sovereigns by acquisition cannot get the right to rule when people surrender to them. Conventions governing tacit consent should thus make sure that they do not sanction coerced consent.

Do states have our tacit consent?

All four general rules should govern social conventions about tacit consent, and it seems that they in fact *do* govern social conventions about tacit consent. But when we want to know if the state's authority is based on tacit consent, what matters is whether there are any conventions actually in place. What could these conventions be? I will discuss three possibilities: (1) that people give tacit consent to the state when they inherit property in line with the laws of the state; (2) that people give tacit consent to the state when they do not emigrate; and (3) that people give tacit consent to the state when they vote.

Locke, as pointed out earlier, believes that states are often founded on explicit consent. But the problem, as he sees it, is that later generations cannot be bound by the founding fathers' explicit consent. His answer is that later generations give tacit consent when they inherit property from their fathers (1689: §§117–22). Yet it seems quite clear that, as a matter of fact, there are no conventions according to which one gives tacit consent to the state and its right to rule by inheriting property. Think back to the case of tacit consent given in the restaurant. The key point here was that there are clear-cut conventions about what counts as tacit consent (it is not entering a restaurant, but ordering a meal) and what is given consent *to* (it is paying the bill, not cleaning up). There are no such conventions regarding the inheritance of property.

And it is not surprising that there are no such conventions. The fourth general rule is quite clearly violated. If refusing one's bequest were required to express dissent, we would have a case of coerced consent: In order to make us "consent" to its authority, the state would put us in the situation where we have to choose between submitting to its authority and obtaining our bequest on the one hand and not submitting to its authority and forgoing our bequest on the other hand. Moreover, the second general rule is also violated, since a convention that would count inheriting property as tacit consent to the state would certainly not be approval-tracking. What inheritors approve of is their bequest (compared to not having it), but this does not imply that they approve of the state (compared to living under no state or living under a different kind of state). Finally, the first general rule also is violated, since the purpose of accepting inherited property is just to receive one's bequest and nothing else.

Does non-emigration fare any better? Harry Beran argues that it does:

> Adults in contemporary states with universal education do know the following propositions. 1. In remaining within the territory of a state when one comes of age one accepts full membership in it. 2. In accepting membership in a rule-governed association (in the absence of coercion, deception, etc.,) one puts oneself under an obligation to obey its rules. 3. The state is a rule-governed association. From 1–3 it follows that 4. In remaining within the territory of a state when one comes of age (in the absence of coercion, deception, etc.) one puts oneself under an obligation to obey its rules. (Beran 1977: 270)

But, as a matter of fact, there are no conventions that count non-emigration as tacit consent to state authority. People are not aware that there is a choice to be made and that they have to emigrate in order to express dissent (Gans 1992: 52; Horton 1992: 33; Simmons 1993: 226–32). The problem thus is the third general rule for conventions governing tacit consent. You are born at a particular place and there is no specific time-point where you are forced to decide whether you would like to stay or go. There is no clear choice situation for anyone.

But, of course, one may try to establish a convention as Beran envisages it and create a clear choice situation. (Beran in later works seems to concede that there *actually* is no such convention.) One could make TV spots that try to establish that accepting the right to vote at age 16 (or some other age) implies accepting membership in the political community and counts as tacit consent to political authority. But there is a problem that speaks against establishing such a convention, and this has to do with the fourth general rule for conventions governing tacit consent. If such a convention were established, one would get coerced consent (Simmons 1979: 95–100; 1993: 232–42; Gans 1992: 53–6; Horton 1992: 34–6; Klosko 2005: 125–9). This point had basically been made by David Hume with a famous analogy (1748): Imagine you are kidnapped and brought on board a ship. Once the ship is far away from the shore in the middle of the ocean, only water and sharks all around, the captain says: "I see that you are still here. If you didn't love it, you'd leave it, and so I take the fact that you're here to be tacit consent to my authority." Obviously, something has gone wrong here, and what is wrong is that we have a case of coerced consent again. The analogy should be clear: The sea and the sharks are not a real option, and while emigration may be an option for some, it involves high financial and emotional costs, costs that are too high for many. Now of course drowning at sea is more costly than emigrating, and there are other important differences between the cases, too. (For example, one is usually not brought to a country against one's will.) But this does not change the main point, which is not so much that the costs are too high, but that we would have a case of coerced consent: In order to make you "consent," the state put you in the situation where you have to choose between either bearing the costs of emigration or submitting to its authority. This is coercive and invalidates any consent the state could get. As Michael Huemer puts it, when we think that the state may ask dissenters to leave, then we presuppose that the state already has political authority in a certain territory; but this cannot be presupposed since it would already need everyone's tacit consent in order to have such authority (2013: 28–30).

Beran has a reply, though. He concedes that a convention that requires emigration to express dissent would be coercive for people who would like to express dissent. But he argues that it is not coercive for everyone who is willing to give consent to political authority anyway, which is the great majority (1987: 101–3). This reply is not convincing, however. First of all, it matters if a minority is coerced into giving invalid consent. It means that the state has no political authority over them, and so we would not be able to explain the holistic nature of political authority (it is to apply to all citizens and everyone in the territory; see p. 7). Second, it may be true that those who would like to give consent anyway are not coerced into giving consent by making emigration the only way to express dissent. But this does not change the fact that the convention for giving tacit consent to the state would be coercive and result in invalid consent.

Beran also proposes to install so-called "dissenters' territories" within a country's borders to make emigration easier and to deal with cases where willing emigrants are not able to find some other country that allows them to immigrate (1977: 269; 1987: 32, 104, 125). Forcing someone to move to a dissenters' territory may be less bad than forcing someone to move to a foreign country. The problem is that it does not make the imposed choice any less coercive. I conclude that one cannot regard continued residence as a sign for tacit consent to political authority.

Voting – and other forms of political participation – is another promising candidate for the locus of tacit consent to political authority (Plamenatz 1938: 167–72; Singer 1974: 45–59; Steinberger 2004: 218–22; Knowles 2010: 113–16). But again there are serious problems (Smith 1973: 962–3; Pateman 1979: 83–91; Beran 1987: 70–7; Greenawalt 1987: 70–3; Horton 1992: 36–8; Klosko 1992: 144–5; Simmons 1993: 218–24). First of all, many people do not vote, and so even if voting could count as tacit consent to the state's authority (Singer calls it "quasi-consent"), a considerable percentage of the population usually does not give that tacit consent. Second, and more importantly, as a matter of fact there are no social conventions according to which voting counts as tacit consent to the state. Again, there are good reasons why there are no such conventions, because such conventions would violate the first general rule. By voting, one may support a certain candidate or a party program and express that one prefers them to alternative candidates or programs; but to express this, one need not take a stance on the very principled question of whether the state should exist at all or whether its claims to authority are warranted.

Summing up, then, there certainly is such a thing as tacit consent, and tacit consent indeed has the power to give rise to new rights (the *explanation condition* is met). But there are no social conventions that would allow people to give the state its right to rule via tacit consent. (Also, there should not be such conventions.) Tacit consent does not help consent theory to meet the *success condition*.

Hypothetical consent

Maybe there is yet another way to ground political authority on consent. Maybe it is sufficient if there is a *hypothetical* storyline in which everyone gives consent (Pitkin 1965; Kavka 1986: Ch. 10; Gaus 2011: 465–70; Weale 2017). A state would then have authority not because people have actually consented, but because they *would* consent in some appropriate hypothetical scenario.

Now at first sight, the proposal to rely on hypothetical consent may seem absurd. Hypothetical consent is obviously very different from real consent, just like hypothetical food is very different from real food. Hypothetical food cannot feed the hungry, and my hypothetical selling of my car cannot actually sell my car. As Ronald Dworkin famously points out, a "hypothetical contract is not simply a pale form of an actual contract; it is no contract at all" (1973: 501).

And yet hypothetical consent matters. It matters because it shows that people would have excellent *reasons* to give consent – even if, as a matter of fact, they do not give consent. As Jeremy Waldron puts it, "we shift our emphasis away from the will and focus on the reasons that people might have for exercising their will in one way rather than another" (1987: 144). So in fact hypothetical consent is not about consent at all. It shows that people would have good reason to give consent to X and that therefore X is *acceptable* to them.

But can the acceptability of the state – or the acceptability of certain kinds of states – explain why these states have the right to rule? It cannot. First of all, it is doubtful that any states enjoy the hypothetical consent of everyone (Horton 1992: 85; Huemer 2013: 48–50). In deeply diverse societies, no type of state will be acceptable to all. The mere fact that there are reasonable anarchists is enough to prove this. Of course one might be able to claim that states have the hypothetical consent of everyone when one uses highly idealized counterparts of real persons in the hypothetical scenario. But such hypothetical consent would no longer tell us much about what is acceptable for real persons.

Second, acceptability can sometimes turn something morally impermissible into something morally permissible.

For example, a physician may proceed with some medical procedure when the patient is in a coma, but would presumably give his consent (if he could). But hypothetical consent rarely grounds duties or obligations (Horton 1992: 85–6; Huemer 2013: 43–5). A job offer might be acceptable for me, and I might have very good reason to accept it, but this does not mean that I have a duty to accept it. If that is so, it is hard to see how it could ground political authority with the power to impose duties on people.

Kavka thinks that an inference from hypothetical consent to certain social arrangements to obligations to comply with the rules of these arrangements works when the hypothetical consent shows not merely that it is acceptable to have these arrangements, but that they are *required* by reason (1986: 401). But, again, even though it may be required by reason for me to accept a job offer, I have no obligation to do so. Maybe this is different when submitting to some arrangement is required by reason because it is my moral duty to submit? This might be a promising thought, but what matters, then, is my moral duty to submit to the arrangement, not the acceptability of the arrangement. I will discuss natural duty-based accounts in Chapter 5.

So let us get back to hypothetical consent as indicating acceptability. Some may still wonder why hypothetical consent cannot ground moral powers, if on the other hand it can sometimes turn something morally impermissible into something morally permissible. Well, that it is acceptable for others if I work on my laptop on the train partly explains why it is permissible for me to do it, but it does not show anything about my powers to impose duties on others. That some medical treatment is acceptable to an unconscious victim of a car accident explains why it is permissible to provide that medical treatment, but it does not tell us anything about powers to impose duties on the victim. And so on. That it is permissible to do these things means that one has liberty-rights to do these things, but liberty-rights are quite different from powers to impose duties on others.

The same holds when we consider not acceptable actions, but acceptable institutions. Imagine an acceptable (or even good) institution, like Oxfam. Its acceptability can show that it would be nice and certainly morally permissible to support

Oxfam, and it can also show that Oxfam permissibly does what it does. But the acceptability of Oxfam does not show that Oxfam has any powers to impose duties on me, for example duties to support them with money.

Having political authority means having powers to impose duties. Without the power to impose duties, states cannot do what they do. Because the acceptability of (certain kinds of) states cannot show that these states have such powers, it cannot establish the state's authority. In other words, hypothetical consent theory does not meet the *explanation condition*.

It should be noted that these problems with hypothetical consent come up when it is used to explain political obligations or political authority. It is much more common to employ the idea of hypothetical consent to justify principles of justice (Rawls 1971) or principles of intersubjective morality more generally (Gauthier 1986; Scanlon 1998), and nothing I have said here is an argument against doing this.

Normative consent

A sophisticated new variant of a hypothetical consent theory has recently been advanced by David Estlund (2008: Ch. 7). Maybe his theory can overcome the problems of traditional hypothetical consent theory. Estlund starts with the observation that consent can sometimes be invalid or "nullified," for example in cases of coerced consent. If consent is invalid, one can proceed as if no consent had been given. Now if consent can sometimes be invalid, *non-consent* might sometimes be invalid as well. One reason why a person's non-consent could be invalid, says Estlund, is that she was morally required to give consent. When a person does not give consent, even though she is morally required to give consent, then her non-consent is nullified and we can proceed as if she had given consent. Instead of saying that people give "nullified non-consent," one can also say that they give "normative consent" (because they were morally required to give consent, but did not do so).

Here is Estlund's example (2008: 124). After an airplane crash, the flight attendant wants to help the injured and says "You! I need you to do as I say!" Because coordinated action is required and the flight attendant is experienced and competent, you are morally required to consent to her authority and to do what she says. Even if you in fact do not consent to her authority, you arguably cannot escape the obligation to do as she says. Whether you consent or not, you have the same obligation as if you had actually given consent, simply because you were morally required to give consent.

The basic idea of normative consent theory can be traced back to Immanuel Kant. Kant is clear that there is no actual consent required for state authority. The "original contract" is an "idea of reason" that both justifies state authority and sets limits to justifiable exercises of state power. The idea of the original contract justifies state authority since everyone has a *moral duty* to enter civil society and realize equal freedom and the rule of law (1793: Sec. 2; 1797: Part I §42). Actual non-consent to the state or particular laws is therefore nullified.

How convincing is Estlund's theory? First, one may doubt that Estlund has given any examples where nullified non-consent establishes authority. In the flight attendant case, for example, it has been argued that the flight attendant does not really have authority, but merely "leadership"; leadership involves a power to impose duties, but with less error tolerance than proper authority (Edmundson 2011: 344–6). I am not sure whether this hits the mark. What seems special about the authority or leadership of the flight attendant is that it is strictly limited in both content and time. It is a very "local" form of practical authority. This is true, but the authority of bosses is usually also more limited than the authority of states, for example. There are different forms of authority and it would be sufficiently interesting if nullified non-consent could establish such limited forms of authority.

A second objection says that the reasons why withholding consent is wrongful are by themselves sufficient to establish authority, such that the idea of nullified non-consent becomes superfluous (Sreenivasan 2009; Koltonski 2013). Why is it wrong to withhold consent to the authority of the flight attendant? Because we have a moral duty to help and submitting to the authority of the flight attendant is necessary to help in an efficient way. If that is so, why not directly say that the flight attendant has authority simply because we have a moral duty to help and submitting to her authority is necessary to help in an efficient way? In other words, Estlund's theory seems to collapse into a natural duty-based account (see Chapter 5).

A third problem for normative consent theory is that an obligation to give consent sometimes quite clearly does *not* nullify non-consent. This is a point Estlund explicitly acknowledges (2008: 126). If, for some reason, I would be morally required to consent to sex (say because I promised to do so), this fact cannot nullify wrongful actual non-consent. My *actual* consent is needed to allow another person to have sex with me, no matter if I am morally required to give such consent or not. It is unclear under what conditions a moral obligation to give consent can nullify actual non-consent and under what conditions it cannot. One idea Estlund tries out is that A's moral obligation to consent to X can only nullify actual non-consent when X does not involve interference with A's person or property. But if that were true, then certainly an obligation to consent to state authority could not ground state authority, since state authority involves the right to coercively enforce laws, which quite clearly means an interference with person and property.

Estlund, though, is prepared to endorse an extremely thin conception of authority. He writes:

> [T]he nullity of nonconsent to authority does not permit anyone to do anything. It does not even permit anyone to issue commands, since all it does is put someone under a duty to obey them if they are issued. Whether it is permissible to issue the commands is a separate question. Since null non-consent to authority only creates authority, and does not permit any actions, then a fortiori it does not permit interference in my person or property. (2008: 127)

But this kind of authority has nothing much to do with political authority. Having political authority means having the liberty-right to enact and coercively enforce laws and the power to impose duties, and if an obligation to consent to coercion cannot help to nullify non-consent to coercion, then it cannot help to establish political authority. Normative consent thus does not help consent theory to meet the *explanation condition*, at least with regard to political authority.

Making states voluntary?

Hypothetical consent cannot establish political authority, but actual consent certainly can. As we have seen, the problem simply is that our states do not have the actual consent of the governed (be it explicit or tacit consent). But would it be possible to rearrange our institutions such that states could actually gain the consent of the governed? Some think it would (de Puydt 1860; Beran 1987: Ch. 7; Simmons 1993: 241–4; Dietrich 2014: 75–6). First of all, the state would have to actually ask citizens whether they would like to consent to the state's authority or not. Once a year, or once in five years, citizens could be required to answer the question whether they give consent to the state's authority, with a "yes" or "no" alternative. This might be done online or with voting machines in regular election offices. The difficulty is to avoid getting invalid coerced consent. To coerce non-consenters to leave the country would invalidate any consent the state could achieve. Thus non-consent has to be made a reasonable alternative. One has to create real exit options *within the state*, so that people can express dissent without having to emigrate or move to "dissenters' territories."

A basic problem is that once you allow exit options within the state, the state will not be able to achieve political authority in the holistic sense; it will not have authority over *all* people in its territory. But let us neglect that problem for a second. What could exit options within the state look like? Non-consenters should be released from legal obligations, as far as possible. So non-consenters would not have to pay taxes, they would not have to serve in the military, they would not have to obey the law on their private ground (they could smoke marijuana even if this is against the law, for example). On the other hand, of course the state could exclude non-consenters from the benefits it provides, as far as this is possible. With non-excludable goods it is not possible. When the state provides national defense, for example, everyone in the territory will benefit from this and no one can be excluded. But some goods are excludable, of course. Thus non-consenters would not be allowed to vote, they would not be allowed to use public transportation, and they would not be allowed to get public health insurance or to attend public universities. Arguably, though, the state would in turn have to allow them to use privately owned public transportation, to build and use private roads, to get private health insurance, and to attend private schools and universities. Otherwise it would coerce people into consenting and thereby invalidate all the consent it could get.

So far, so good. Would a voluntary state also have to allow dissenters to use private police forces and private courts? If it does *not* allow for private police companies and private courts, then it has two options in how to deal with crimes against non-consenters. First, it could leave them unprotected and not allow them to bring their case to state courts. If the state did that, then of course non-consent to the state would not be a viable option, and all the consent the state could get would again become coerced consent and thus invalid. Second, it could grant normal police protection and access to courts for non-consenters. But this would make it highly attractive for citizens to leave the state in order to get peace, security, and law and order for free. For that reason, probably very many people would not give consent to the state and thus would leave it without financial support, and this would probably mean that the state would eventually collapse (see Klosko 2005: 132, 136, 138–40).

So it seems that a voluntary state indeed has to allow for private police forces and private courts for non-consenters. But if the state allows for private police forces and courts, then it not only gives up any claims to holistic political authority, it also renounces its monopoly on the use of force. It thereby *stops being a state* and becomes one service provider among others.

Making our states consensual organizations via institutional reform is therefore illusionary. If consent is really required for having states with legitimate political authority, then we have to conclude that our present and very probably all future states lack legitimate political authority. What to make of this conclusion will be discussed in Chapter 7.

One final thought: There might be a very different way to make states consensual, at least to a certain degree. One could relax the requirement of consent and treat it not as a strict requirement for state authority, but as an *ideal*. Amanda Greene explains why a consensual state is an ideal

(2016: 92): "When voluntary rule is achieved, there is at least some partial alignment between what an individual values and what goods are promoted by the political order to which he is subject." States, according to her, can be more or less legitimate, depending on the proportion of people that consent (2016: 87). Grossly uninformed consent does not count, though, because it does not achieve the said alignment between what an individual values and what the state actually does (2016: 85).

Now the first thing to note is that rights are not scalar, but binary; one either has a right or one lacks it. So if the ideal of a voluntary state is to explain the right to rule and hence political authority, there has to be a threshold of support at which the state gets the right to rule. But every such threshold would look arbitrary; why should a state that enjoys the consent of 67 percent of its subjects have the right to rule, while a state that enjoys the consent of 66 percent does not, for example? Second, treating consent as a mere ideal simply does not explain how some people can come to have the right to rule over non-consenting equals. Accordingly, some advocates of the ideal of a consensual state feel free to simply ascribe political obligations to those who do not consent (Walzer 1970), or regard them as "political children" that may be governed without consent (Tussman 1960: 36–7). I conclude that treating consent as an ideal does not meet the *explanation condition*.

Summary

Consent could well explain how new rights and hence political authority have come into being. Unfortunately, our states actually do not have everyone's consent (whether explicit or tacit). If consent were necessary for state authority, all states would therefore lack political authority. Neither is it possible to achieve consensual states via institutional reform. Mere hypothetical consent or normative consent, on the other hand, cannot explain political authority.

3
The Service Conception of Authority

The service conception of authority has been devised by Joseph Raz. Its basic idea is to conceive authorities as a service for those who submit to them. It is an intriguing theory because it promises to account for all sorts of authority, from the authority of experts to the authority of parents and state officials. The service conception encompasses a theory about how authority should be exercised, a theory about how authority-based reasons work, and a theory about the justification of authority.

How to exercise authority

I start with the first part of the theory, how authority should be exercised. Authority, according to the service conception, is to be understood as a valuable *instrument* for those subject to it. They do better by following the advice or command of the authority. According to the service conception, the role and primary function of authorities is "to serve the governed" (Raz 1986: 56). It is to serve them by helping them to believe or do what they have reason to believe or do. Accordingly, authority should be exercised in line with the reasons that apply to the subject independently of the authoritative directives. As Raz puts it: "[A]ll authoritative directives should be based on reasons which already independently apply to the subjects of the directives and are relevant to their action in the circumstances covered by the directive" (1986: 47). This is what Raz calls the *dependence thesis*. It is a normative thesis about how authority should be exercised. Of course it is not a thesis about what (de facto) authorities actually do. It is about what they should do.

Obviously, the *dependence thesis* is fairly abstract. The reasons that apply to a subject (and that the authority should base its directives on) can be of very different kinds. Sometimes an authority helps the subject to better further his or her own interests or well-being; sometimes the authority helps the subjects to follow the moral reasons that apply.

The interesting point is that the *dependence thesis* is to hold for all different kinds of authority. All authorities are to "serve the governed." In that sense, the service conception scores very high on the *target condition* (see p. 15), since it promises a unified account of all different forms of authority. The *dependence thesis* is certainly highly plausible for theoretical authorities. Opera experts and physicians can give bad advice on purpose, but this obviously is not what they should do. They should indeed help people who need their authority. A physician, for example, should advise the patient to take a particular antibiotic just in the case when the patient has good reasons to do so, usually because taking the antibiotic promises to restore the patient's health. If asked which recording of *Tosca* one should buy, an expert in Puccini operas should give advice in light of what he thinks the best recording is. In other words, he should give advice in light of the reasons that apply to people who are interested in purchasing a good recording of *Tosca* (independently of the advice of the expert).

How about practical authorities? Should they also base their directives on reasons that apply to their subjects independently of the directives? In the case of parents, the answer is "yes." It is quite intuitive to think that parents' authoritative directives should be a service to their children. For example, when a father orders his daughter to do her homework, then this is because doing her homework will help her succeed at school, which again will help her in her adult life. It is also plausible to conceive the authority of school teachers as a service to the children. Indeed, while consent theory can be understood as a theory that takes bosses and employees as the paradigm of proper – because consensual – relations of authority, the service conception can be understood as taking parents and children (or maybe teachers and children) as the paradigm of proper – because serviceable – relations of authority.

But the *dependence thesis* looks less plausible when it comes to the authority of bosses and the authority of states and their officials. Here it is harder to see in what sense authoritative directives could be a service to the governed. To understand how these forms of authority can be conceived as a service, it is important to recall that an authority need not base its directives on reasons that further the subject's personal interests. Even supporters of workplace democracy may concede that some sort of bossism is usually unavoidable for leading a successful firm. If we assume that an employee has reason to contribute to the success of the firm, then a boss who gives directives with an eye to the success of the firm can be said to base her directives on reasons that independently apply to the employee. Insofar as a boss should also care about the well-being of the employees, she should of course also base her directives on considerations about the well-being of the employees. The same holds with reasons that relate to the social and ecological responsibility of the firm: When a boss gives directives with an eye to this responsibility, she looks at reasons that again apply to the employee independently of the directives.

The same holds for states and state officials. A judge in a civil law case provides a service to the parties that take their argument to the court. The judge should decide the case in light of the facts and so of the reasons that apply to the parties independently of his judgment. No matter how he decides, the arbitration service will serve the parties. One thing that can be learned from this case, therefore, is that the reasons that the authority takes into account (the merits of the case) need not be identical with the parties' reasons to submit to an authority and to follow the directive of the authority (their need for an arbiter) (Viehoff 2011: 257–8).

Of course, states do much more than providing civil courts. But other activities can be reconstructed as a service, too: When the state enacts a law against murder, then of course this law can be regarded as based on reasons that apply to everyone independently of the law, namely on moral reasons not to murder. And so on.

Is there anyone who thinks that authorities may disregard the reasons that apply to those who are subject to the authoritative directives? How could one oppose the *dependence thesis*? One objection – discussed by Raz himself (1986: 45–6) – is that sometimes there are no antecedent independent reasons that would apply to the subjects. Before tax laws are enacted, for example, citizens do not have any reasons to pay taxes. Does this speak against the *dependence thesis*? Well, of course one could say that even before tax laws are enacted subjects have reasons to support certain causes that are advanced by taxes, or that they have reasons to in general support reasonably just states. In that sense, one can always come up with relevant reasons that apply to the citizens before the authority's directive. The *dependence thesis*, then, looks pretty plausible, if not trivial.

How authority-based reasons work

Authority should be a service to the governed, according to Raz. To better understand the service conception we should now discuss how authority-based reasons are supposed to work compared to other reasons for action or belief. By authority-based reasons, I mean the reasons that are constituted by an authority's order, advice, or opinion. These reasons can be either reasons for belief or reasons for action. When an expert on opera offers her opinion on an opera performance, people have reason to believe that her judgment is true or at least illuminating. When a physician gives advice on what medicine to take, one has reason to do as he says.

How do these authority-based reasons work? If we focus on practical authorities, the first thing to note is that authority-based reasons do not merely provide information about the reasons that apply independently to the agent. According to

The Service Conception of Authority 41

Raz, an authority's directive *makes a difference* to the balance of reasons (1986: 29–30, 48–51, 67). An authority, just by say-so, can *add* something to the balance of reasons. Take traffic laws, for example, like a law to drive on the right-hand side of the street. That the state orders drivers to drive on the right is not informative about an alleged independent reason to drive on the right. It constitutes all by itself a reason to drive on the right. This shows that a practical authority's power to impose duties is not a mere side-effect power (see p. 11): When an authority orders something, it creates a content-independent new reason for action by mere say-so.

How does all this fit with the *dependence thesis* from above? Did not the *dependence thesis* say that authorities have to give directives with an eye to the reasons that independently apply to the subjects? How can directives be made in light of reasons that apply independently, but on the other hand do more than inform about these reasons? Well, in the case of traffic laws, for example, the state should indeed base its directives on reasons that apply independently on the subject; but, of course, people do not have a reason to drive on any particular side of the street without the directive of the state (or some other institution or convention). They have reason to drive in a *well-coordinated manner*, and this is what the state should look at when giving directives about how to drive. Or take the case of tax laws again. Here quite obviously the state does not inform the citizens about reasons to pay taxes that apply independently of the state's directives. There are no reasons to pay taxes without tax laws, since it is not even possible to pay taxes without tax laws and the relevant fiscal authorities. Nevertheless, the state should give tax laws with an eye to reasons that apply independently to the citizens, like reasons to support the state's functioning or to support particular tasks of the state.

There are two caveats, though. First, when a practical authority gives a directive that merely specifies a pre-existing duty, it does not seem to add *much* to the balance of reasons. When, for example, the state enacts a law against murder, then the balance of reasons has not changed much. In addition to the moral duty not to commit murder, people now also have a legal duty not to commit murder (Sherman 2010: 426–7). Nevertheless, one can insist that it *does* add an additional reason and is not merely informing about the balance of reasons. Second, that authority-based reasons are more than informative only holds for practical authorities. Theoretical authorities, for example experts on nineteenth-century opera, indeed provide reasons that merely inform about the balance of reasons, but do not add anything to the balance of reasons (see Raz 1986: 29).

I asked how authority-based reasons work. The first point was that they do more than informing about the balance of reasons: They *change* the balance of reasons (although this is not true in the case of theoretical authorities). The second point is that authority-based reasons are *pre-emptive* reasons. Authority-based reasons do not merely change the balance of reasons by adding another reason to the balance of reasons; they *take the place* of other reasons that apply to the agent. An agent follows an authority when she takes the directives of the authority as binding, such that she ignores what she might personally think she should do. In that sense, authority-based reasons replace other reasons. Raz's *pre-emption thesis* thus says: "[T]he fact that an authority requires performance of an action is a reason for its performance which is not to be added to all other relevant reasons when assessing what to do, but should exclude and take the place of some of them" (1986: 46).

Let me illustrate the *pre-emption thesis* with different kinds of authorities, starting with theoretical authorities. When I learn something about opera from Carolyn Abbate's and Roger Parker's book, I should take that piece of information or judgment as a reason for belief that replaces reasons to believe otherwise that I might have entertained before (see Raz 2006: 1033). This, at least, is what I do when I take them as authoritative. Likewise, when I think that I just have a light cold and can easily spend the day working, but my doctor says that I have the flu and should stay in bed and sleep all day, then I treat her as an authority when I stay in bed and ignore my own assessment of the matter. Same with practical authorities: When a police officer says that I may not continue driving, this is not just one reason among others that co-determines what I should do. I can no longer make a decision based on what I think the overall balance of reasons is. If I take the officer's directive as authoritative, her order replaces other reasons that might apply.

Relatedly, the *pre-emption thesis* can explain in what sense laws and rules can be called "authoritative" (and hence talk of the "authority of law"), even though laws and rules obviously cannot have rights (only people can). Rules and laws can be regarded as authoritative when they should be taken as binding and hence as replacing the reasons that apply to the agents independently of the rules (Raz 1979: Ch. 2; 1986: 57–9).

Two clarifications are important. First, the *pre-emption thesis* does not imply that one has to follow an authority's directives come what may. It just explains what it means to exercise authority and to follow authority. There are two kinds of cases where an agent should not follow an authority. One is the case of an illegitimate de facto authority. People take it as authoritative, but it is not. The other is the case of a legitimate authority that errs on a particular point and gives a bad directive. Usually, one should follow the directives of legitimate authorities even when one thinks they are bad, because otherwise there would be no point in submitting to the authority in the first place (Raz 1986: 47, 60–1; 2006: 1022–3). But sometimes, when an otherwise legitimate authority gives morally deeply problematic orders, one ought not to take that directive as authoritative. Note that the *pre-emption thesis* does not say that authority-based reasons should exclude and take the place of *all* other reasons that apply to the agent, but only *some* of them. Some reasons that are *still* taken into account by the agent may speak in favor of not submitting to the authority.

Second, depending on what kind of authority is at stake, one may have or not have a *duty* to follow an authority's directives (Sherman 2010: 424–6). When introducing the *pre-emption thesis*, Raz has practical authorities in mind, authorities with "the power to require action" (1986: 38). When we consider theoretical authorities, i.e. authorities who have great knowledge in a certain realm, people usually do not have a duty to follow their advice. Correspondingly, such authorities are usually not in a position to give orders. A physician, for example, usually offers advice, and the patient does not have a duty to follow. To be sure, the patient should take the physician's advice as a pre-emptive reason for action that replaces other reasons. But only practical authorities have the power to impose duties on people; it is only here that pre-emptive reasons come in the form of duties.

An objection against the *pre-emption thesis* says that *if* it is essential for legitimate authorities to provide pre-emptive reasons, then there might not *be* any legitimate authorities, because it is either irrational or immoral or both to take directives as pre-emptive. Why is that? Well, maybe because as human beings we ought to make up our own minds and decide autonomously what we should do (see Wolff 1970; Hurd 1991). This does not mean that we should never take the advice of experts. But in the end, we should always consider the balance of reasons for ourselves. This objection, though, exaggerates the conflict between autonomy and authority. Take arbitrators. Arbitrators can only function as arbitrators if their clients take their directives as binding, and of course people need arbitrators on many occasions. This does not seem to undermine people's autonomy. Moreover, as explained before, the *pre-emption thesis* does not claim that we should always follow legitimate authorities, come what may. There are occasions when one should not follow them.

Still, the objection makes an important point. It often seems rational not to take an authority's directive or advice as a pre-emptive reason (Himma 2007: 125–8, 131–3). When you would like to buy a recording of Verdi's *Falstaff*, then you certainly do well to consider the advice of Carolyn Abbate and Roger Parker; but you can well take their advice as one consideration among others, and in the end assess the balance of reasons for yourself. Now one may say that you do not treat them as an authority if you assess the balance of reasons for yourself, but this seems to be an artificially narrow picture of what authorities are. The pre-emption thesis, then, does not seem to be true of all authority-based reasons. Indeed Raz seems to agree that one need not take experts as providing pre-emptive reasons (2010: 300–1). An authority provides pre-emptive reasons mainly if some kind of coordination or arbitration is needed. This obviously narrows the applicability of the pre-emption thesis considerably. Only some authorities provide pre-emptive reasons; many do not.

The justification of authority

So far I have laid out the service conception's view of how authority should be exercised (it should be based on reasons that apply to the subject independently of authoritative directives) and how authority-based reasons work (they are pre-emptive and more than informative, at least on some occasions). What is most interesting in the context of this book is how we can justify authority: What has to be the case for someone to have legitimate authority? The service conception provides an answer that is closely related to the *pre-emption thesis* and the *dependence thesis*.

Consent theory claimed that practical authorities need the consent of the governed in order to be legitimate. (Parents and school teachers were exceptions because children cannot give valid consent to authority.) Valid consent was conceived as a necessary and sufficient condition for the legitimacy of these types of authority. What does the service conception say? The answer comes in the form of Raz's *normal justification thesis*:

> The normal way to establish that a person has authority over another person involves showing that the alleged subject is likely better to comply with reasons which already independently apply to him [...] if he accepts the directives of the alleged authority as authoritatively binding and tries to follow them, rather than by trying to follow the reasons which apply to him directly. (1986: 53)

Legitimate authorities really are a service to their subjects (and do not merely pretend to be). If people do better by submitting to an authority than by trying to figure out what to do by themselves, then the authority is legitimate. The account specifies *who* is an authority, over *whom* he is an authority, and with *regard to what* things he is an authority.

The *normal justification thesis* is coined for practical authorities, like parents, bosses, teachers, state officials, and religious leaders: Authorities that have the power to impose duties on people. Theoretical authorities cannot impose duties on people. As Raz notes, these authorities are not even properly said to have authority "over us" (2006: 1034).

Nevertheless, something similar to the *normal justification thesis* could also be formulated for theoretical authorities (Zagzebski 2012). Arguably, someone is a theoretical authority relative to some subject when submitting to his or her judgment helps that subject to believe what she should believe or do what she should do.

Objections against the normal justification thesis

There are two important objections against the *normal justification thesis*. The first objection applies to the *normal justification thesis* as a claim about *political* authority. This objection says that the thesis fails to take account of the procedural and in particular the democratic sources of legitimate political authority (Waldron 1999: Ch. 5; Hershovitz 2003; Christiano 2004: 279–80; Himma 2007: 142–4; Schmelzle 2015: 140–9). Because we disagree about what reasons there are in politics and about what good or just laws would be, democratic procedures are essential to political authority. Yet in reply, one can argue that Raz's service conception can well account for the procedural dimension of democracies, since providing fair arbitration procedures is precisely a service as envisaged by Raz's theory (Viehoff 2011). It is a different question whether democratic procedures can by themselves explain political authority. I will get back to this in Chapter 5.

A second and in my view stronger objection is that the *normal justification thesis* fails to specify sufficient conditions for the moral power to impose duties and the liberty-right to enforce them that is essential for all forms of practical authority including political authority (Perry 2005: 280–3; Himma 2007: 140–2; Darwall 2009; 2010; Quong 2011: Ch. 4). That I would do better by following the directives of my dentist does not imply that my dentist has the moral power to impose duties on me and the moral liberty to coercively enforce them. Jonathan Quong presents the case of a tour company that offers by far the best tours of Peru at a reasonable price (2011: 108–9). I might best follow the reasons that apply to me if I book a tour with them and follow their directives. Yet it seems that the company does not have moral powers over me as long as I do not actually book a tour with them. In particular, the fact that I would do better if I went with them does not give the tour company the moral power to impose duties on me, like a duty to pay them, for example. Since it lacks a power to impose duties, it also lacks the liberty to coercively enforce these duties, of course. Providing a good service, then, is not sufficient for having rights to impose and coercively enforce duties.

A first reply is that the *normal justification thesis* can be used separately for different aspects of authority. It could show that someone has the power to impose duties, but not to coercively enforce these duties, for example. Raz writes:

> That an authority is entitled to impose a duty to F does not entail that it is entitled to impose a sanction for failing to F, or a remedy should any right be violated thereby. One needs a separate argument for that, and the argument – on my account – would be provided if [*the normal justification thesis*] would apply to those additional measures. (2010: 300)

Similarly, sometimes the *normal justification thesis* may only show that someone is a theoretical authority (i.e. an expert in some field or good at doing something), but does not have the power to impose duties. So far, so good. But one can stipulate that I would indeed better comply with reasons that apply to me independently of authoritative directives if the tour company could coerce me to comply with its commands. Once they brought me to Peru, I would see that it was good that they forced me on to their tour. Yet the tour company still does not seem to have the right to coerce me on to their tour, and so the first answer does not help to avoid the counterintuitive result that the tour company does have that right.

A second reply is that the *normal justification thesis* is not even supposed to specify sufficient conditions for legitimate authority. There are further necessary conditions for legitimate authority that are not satisfied in the tour company example. One is that only entities that *claim* to have authority could actually have authority (Raz 2006: 1005). Since the tour company does not claim authority, it cannot have legitimate authority. This is true, and yet it seems that the tour company would lack authority even if it *did* claim to have authority.

Another necessary condition has to do with the value of independent decision-making. Raz makes clear that "the desirability of people conducting their own life by their own lights" can sometimes be more important than receiving the service an alleged authority could provide (1986: 57). He later calls this the "independence condition" (2006: 1014). The tour company example could thus be a case in point, where the independence condition explains why the tour company has no legitimate authority even though I would do better by complying with its directives. This reply is good, as far as it goes, but unless we are told under what conditions people should be conducting their own life by their own lights, even though submitting to an authority would be a service to them, the *normal justification thesis* is rather uninformative. In the end, it comes down to this: "The normal way to establish that a person has authority over another person involves showing that the alleged subject is likely better to comply with reasons which already independently apply to him if he accepts the directives of the alleged authority as authoritatively binding and tries to follow them, rather than by trying to follow the reasons which apply to him directly, *except when this does not establish that the person has authority*." The service conception could at best be one part of a theory that explains how persons can come to have authority over others, specifying one necessary condition among others. (Of course one could also have doubts that being serviceable is even a necessary condition for having authority; maybe valid consent is sufficient.) By itself, the service conception does not establish that someone has authority. In that sense, then, the service conception does not satisfy the *explanation condition*.

But let us put this objection against the *normal justification thesis* to one side and assume that the thesis is correct and has explanatory power. There is a third worry, then, namely that the *normal justification thesis* cannot show that at least some actual states have political authority (see Raz 1986: 74–8). At best, states could have varying degrees of authority over their citizens. What authority they have would depend on whether a particular citizen needs certain state activities as a service or not. States would have more authority over one person than over another, and might well have no authority over some persons at all. Our states, on the other hand, claim a quite general right to rule over all citizens and persons in their territory (this is what I called the holistic nature of political authority; see p. 7). In that sense, the service conception cannot establish political authority as it is usually understood, and so it fails to meet the *success condition*, too.

Summary

The service conception conceives authorities as a service for those who submit to them. It encompasses a theory about how authority should be exercised, a theory about how authority-based reasons work, and a theory about the justification of authority. According to the last of these, one has legitimate authority if those who are subject to one's authority thereby better comply with reasons which already independently apply to them. The problem is that this fails to specify sufficient conditions for someone's moral power to impose duties and the liberty-right to enforce them, and thus the service conception cannot explain political authority on its own. Moreover, even neglecting that problem, the service conception cannot account for the holistic nature of political authority.

4
Community and Authority

Community-based justifications of political authority are the most straightforward ones. According to such justifications, political communities can be conceived by analogy to families. Just like there are moral bonds within families, there also are moral bonds within political communities, and these bonds include relations of authority.

Moral bonds in families

So let us start with families. We all believe that we have moral bonds with other family members, most clearly with our parents, children, and siblings, but also with less close relatives. These bonds are not emotional bonds, although of course there usually are emotional bonds, too; they are *moral* bonds which constitute moral obligations and rights. For example, as sons and daughters, we have moral obligations to support our parents when they get old and need our help. Obviously, this is not to say that the only reason to support them is that we have such obligations; if things go well, we support them because we love them. But the point is that we also feel that this is what we morally ought to do, that we would be morally blameworthy if we did not support them. As parents, we have moral obligations to raise and educate our children appropriately. Again, this is not to say that there are no excellent other reasons to raise and educate our children appropriately. If things go well, we raise and educate them as well as we can because we love them. But, again, we also feel that this is what we morally ought to do, and that we would be morally culpable if we failed to do so. Pointing out moral obligations does not mean saying that people should be primarily motivated by such obligations. The same holds for our brothers and sisters, and – to a lesser extent – for grandparents, uncles and aunts, etc. There is a sense of connection that most people feel is natural among family members.

The idea that we have familial obligations "is one of the most salient moral beliefs we have" (Hardimon 1994: 342). If we have moral beliefs that we are very certain about and could not give up without giving up our sense of who we are, these certainly include beliefs about moral bonds within families. Indeed we are so certain about moral obligations in families that they do not seem to require any further explanation; they seem to be morally basic.

It should be noted that biology is not decisive for the issue of familial obligations. Marriage usually counts as a way to become a member of a new family – the family of one's spouse. Adoption is a way to become a member of a new family. Relatedly, the *strength* of familial moral bonds depends on many different factors, and biology is just one among others in this regard. Biology matters, to be sure. That someone is one's biological aunt or cousin arguably constitutes some moral bonds; but more important is whether someone takes a certain familial *role*, in particular the role of a father or mother, brother or sister, and this is not necessarily the biological father, mother, brother, or sister. Moreover, the strength of familial moral bonds depends on how the connection between two persons is in real life, on the actual relationship (see Seglow 2013: Ch. 2). If someone has a close relationship with one's aunt, then the moral bonds arguably grow stronger than they usually are between aunt and nephew or niece. Conversely, if personal relationships are disrupted, the moral bonds become weaker than usual. In extreme cases, the moral bonds even disappear. When children are seriously mistreated by their parents, for example, their obligations to support their parents arguably vanish.

The existence of familial moral bonds can be regarded as a moral puzzle, even though we are so certain that familial moral bonds exist. They can be regarded as a moral puzzle because they imply a partiality that seems to be inimical to any universalist picture of morality with its emphasis on impartiality. On a universalist view of morality, all moral duties and obligations are either universal – owed to all other persons – *or* voluntarily incurred by means of promises, contracts, and the like. Familial obligations seem alien to this view of morality. As Michael Hardimon puts it (before defending familial obligations), there is a "horror at the thought of being *impressed* – like the seamen of old – into social roles and burdened with their attendant obligations against our will" (1994: 347). Familial and other partial obligations smack of a pre-enlightened, tribal view of morality that is to be overcome.

Of course there have been attempts by advocates of universalist ethical theories to accommodate the moral bonds in families, friendships, and political communities (Railton 1984; Goodin 1985: Ch. 5; 1988; Wellman 2000; Blake 2001; Stilz 2009). Thus Peter Railton has argued that our partiality toward our loved ones is justifiable on a consequentialist basis (1984). A sophisticated consequentialist is committed to what Railton calls "objective consequentialism." She wants to live a life that is justifiable from an impartial consequentialist point of view, but she is not committed to "subjective consequentialism" and thus rejects impartial consequentialist reasoning in her everyday life. A sophisticated consequentialist cannot even bring herself to impartial consequentialist reasoning when her loved ones are involved. The clue is that she has an objectively consequentialist justification for this: The world is a better place, from an impartial point of view, when people take special care for their families and friends. A sophisticated consequentialist can thus have true friendships and is not alienated from her deepest personal concerns. Railton's theory has been challenged (Badhwar 1991), and indeed it seems that a sophisticated consequentialist still has to condemn her actions as morally wrong when they favor her loved ones and are suboptimal from an impartial consequentialist perspective (in a particular situation). This is still counterintuitive. Some, therefore, argue that there are moral bonds that are partial *all the way down* (Miller 1995: Ch. 3; Mason 1997; Scheffler 1997; Keller 2013; Seglow 2013). For the purposes of this chapter, it is not terribly important whether we believe that all partial moral bonds can in the end be based on impartial moral principles, or whether we endorse the view that some partial moral bonds cannot be based on such principles. What matters is that there are moral bonds among family members, and that we are so certain about this that we do not seem to *need* to find any deeper grounding or justification for them.

So let us assume that indeed there are moral bonds within families, moral bonds that need no deeper explanation and thus can serve as a starting point in ethical reasoning. What has all this to do with *authority*? Moral bonds within families do not only consist in moral obligations. Parents also have powers with regard to their children, and these powers constitute their parental authority. Parents have the power to make decisions about medical affairs concerning their children, for example (see Cherry 2010). Parents also have the power to impose duties on their children. When a mother tells her fourteen-year-old son to go pick up a parcel for her at the post office or to be home at 10pm, then he arguably has a duty to pick up the parcel or to be home at 10pm, just because his mother said so. Parental authority is as salient as moral obligations in families are. It is part and parcel of the moral landscape as we know it.

It should be noted that parental authority is not unlimited, of course (see Gheaus 2017). A father cannot impose a duty on his daughter to assist him in a bank robbery or to make erotic photos. It is a power to impose duties within a certain range. It is no different from political authority in this regard.

Furthermore, parents cannot impose duties on children before they reach a certain age. Of course, a mother can tell her four-year-old daughter not to do something, but it would be odd to say that the daughter therefore has an obligation not to do it. In order to have obligations, one has to be able to understand what an obligation is. Dogs do not have obligations, even though one can give orders to dogs. It does not matter, for our purposes, at what age a kid is usually able to understand the idea of an obligation. Teens, at least, usually seem to understand what obligations are.

As in the case of moral bonds in families in general, we may ask about the deeper basis for parental authority in particular. Of course the service conception could be cited as a foundation for parental authority: Parents are then said to have authority over their children because and as long as this is a service to the children. But, within the context of the present argument, we can stay agnostic about this. Community-based arguments are trying to convince us that we *need no deeper explanation* for parental authority. We just know that parents have authority over their children. We do not need to find a deeper justification for parental authority to be assured that parents have parental authority. We could *test* ethical theories by asking whether they can accommodate familial bonds including parental authority. If they cannot, we are willing to drop the theory, not our conviction that parents have authority over their children.

In a way, a community-based account of authority thus tries to circumvent my *explanation condition* (see p. 15). Let us accept – for the sake of the argument – that a community-based argument has a great deal of plausibility with regard to parental authority. The question is whether it is also plausible when it comes to political authority. A community-based argument for political authority claims that we can treat political authority as analogous to parental authority, and assume moral bonds among compatriots like we can assume moral bonds among family members. If the analogy holds, we do not need a deeper explanation for political authority.

Political communities as analogous to families

What speaks in favor of treating political communities as analogues to families (and hence to refrain from asking for a deeper explanation of the authority relations within them)? Before starting with some considerations in favor of the analogy, it should be noted that most advocates of community-based arguments have focused on political obligations and not directly on political authority. Because they take one's association with others in a political community as the key to political obligations, they often speak of "associative obligations." But of course political obligations and political authority are related. It is *possible* for people to have political obligations *without* a state that has the authority to impose duties on them, but from the point of view of community-based arguments this seems rather implausible. For that reason, I here take such arguments as arguments for both political obligations and political authority at the same time. I mostly speak of "moral bonds" because this expression can cover all kinds of moral relations, including both obligations and authority.

One thing that speaks in favor of the analogy between family and political communities is that many people seem to be *as certain* about moral bonds in political communities as they are about moral bonds in families. Just like everyone takes it for granted that parents have an obligation to care for their children and to properly educate them, and that children have an obligation to support their parents when they get old and need their help, most people take it for granted that citizens have an obligation to pay taxes, to obey the law, and to vote. The same holds for authority relations. Most people think that *of course* the state has the right to enact and coercively enforce laws and *of course* it has the power to thereby impose duties on citizens. There are not many people who question political authority, just like there are not many people who question parental authority. Some political philosophers have argued that the ideas of political obligations and political authority just belong to our concept of a political society (Macdonald 1941; McPherson 1967).

Second, many people indeed feel connected to their compatriots in a way similar to how they feel connected to members of their family (Horton 1992; Tamir 1993). People identify themselves as members of families and as members of nations and/or states. Some may be willing to deny that, but on reflection they often have to confess that they feel pride or shame for their family or their country (or for particular family members or particular compatriots). Being on vacation abroad, one can easily feel shame for the behavior of one's drunken compatriots, just like one can feel ashamed of the behavior of one's parents or siblings. Watching the Olympics, one can feel pride in the achievements of athletes from one's country, just like one can be proud of the achievements of one's sister. As John Horton remarks, an American citizen who opposed the war in Iraq felt different than a French citizen who opposed the war in Iraq, simply because the United States were involved, but France was not (1992: 171). This connection to family and country can deeply affect one's life. Imagine being a grandniece of Hermann Göring, for example.

When speaking of "compatriots," I deliberately leave open whether this means other members of one's nation – no matter if this nation has a state or not – or whether it means other members of one's state – no matter if this state is multinational or not. Catalans, for example, do not have a state, but arguably are a nation with members living in Spain and in France. Identification and feelings of connectedness sometimes are complicated and can apply to one's nation or state or both. This is no different in families. I usually speak of "political communities," a term that is open enough to allow both interpretations.

An interesting issue is how much weight we should give to objective and subjective aspects in identification (Horton 1992: 183–8). When persons are identified as members of a family or a political community by others and self-identify as members of this family or political community, things are easy. But what happens to moral bonds when people are identified as members of a family or political community by others, but do not self-identify as such members? Does it mean that the moral bonds of family or political community vanish? What, on the other hand, happens when people identify themselves as members of a family or political community, but are not accepted as members by the family or political community (and are not identified as members by outsiders)? Arguably self-identification cannot be sufficient for the existence of moral bonds including authority relations: One must actually *be* a member of a political community or family, and one cannot all alone decide about membership. Membership depends on conventions that are – in some way – under the control of the group. Objective membership is thus at least a necessary condition for the existence of moral bonds. Could it also be sufficient? Arguably it cannot. The subjective aspect, i.e. self-identification, matters, too (see van der Vossen 2011: 490). No one should be stuck in a family or political community; it must be possible to leave one's family and one's political community. Yael Tamir strongly emphasizes this subjective aspect. She writes that associative obligations "must be based on some sense of belonging, on an active and conscious discovery of one's position, and on an affirmation of this position" (1993: 135). But self-identification alone cannot be sufficient for the existence of moral bonds. One also has to be acknowledged as a member. This is especially clear when the moral bonds come in the form of authority relations. Self-identifying as a father of a child is not sufficient for having parental authority, when the rest of the family including the child does not acknowledge my fatherhood. (Of course, things get more complicated again when the person *in fact* is the biological father.) Self-identifying as the king of Sweden certainly does not give me the political authority the king of Sweden has. Is self-identification *necessary* for moral bonds? Arguably not. A father can owe moral obligations to his son even though he does not self-identify as a father. It seems, then, that objective identification is necessary but not sufficient for moral bonds, and that subjective identification is neither necessary nor sufficient, but can matter under certain conditions.

If political authority can be treated as analogous to parental authority, why not treat other forms of authority as analogous to parental authority as well? Why not bosses or religious authorities, teachers or even theoretical authorities? An answer to this question is necessary if the approach is to satisfy the *target condition*. One has to explain why the approach applies to some forms of authority, but not to others. Community-based arguments are limited to parental and political community because other forms of authority are not relevantly similar. Theoretical authorities have nothing to do with special relationships or community, and the authority of bosses is based on voluntary consent in a way that parental and political authority is not. Yet the authority of religious leaders might be relevantly similar to the authority of parents. Insofar as one is born in a religious group, and insofar as people identify as members of religious groups, there might indeed be a case for a community-based argument for the authority of religious leaders. I cannot discuss this issue any further here. The same holds for the authority of school teachers. Insofar as children are expected to go to schools, the authority of their teachers might be understood as a community-based form of authority. The authority of other teachers – like an adult's piano teacher – is based on consent, though. In any case, I do not think that community-based arguments for authority have a problem with the *target condition*. They promise to encompass a wide range of authorities and are quite attractive for that reason.

Summing up, then, there are some good reasons to treat political communities as analogues to families. First, many people are just as certain about moral bonds and authority relations in political communities as they are about moral bonds and authority relations in families. Second, people identify and are identified with their country or nation, just as they identify and are identified with their families.

Objections and refinements

There are several worries or objections about community-based arguments for authority. The first of them applies to community-based arguments for authority in general; the other three apply to community-based arguments for *political* authority in particular. The first worry is that there obviously are deeply unjust or otherwise immoral communities, be it political communities or families (Simmons 1996a: 85; Dagger 2000: 110–12; see also Vernon 2007). Quite obviously, people do not have moral obligations within such communities and there are no authority relations within such communities. A mother who abuses her son loses her parental authority, and a brutal dictator loses his political authority. This can be taken to show that membership in families and political communities alone does not ground moral bonds including authority relations. Advocates of community-based arguments for both parental and political authority need an answer to this worry.

Tamir bites the bullet; she argues that there are moral bonds even in morally reprehensible groups like the Mafia; it is just that these moral obligations are easily overridden by other moral concerns (1993: 101–2). But arguably a father cannot impose a duty on his son to rob the next bank with him. There is not a duty that gets overridden, but no overriding going on at all (Mason 1997: 438; Dagger 2000: 111; van der Vossen 2011: 489).

Margaret Gilbert's solution is to "de-moralize" obligations (2013: Ch. 17). If obligations within immoral communities are not moral obligations, then their existence surely becomes more plausible. But, on the other hand, if obligations are not understood as moral obligations, they do not help us with our task of explaining legitimate authority relations and in particular legitimate political authority.

A better answer to the first worry is to simply claim that certain moral criteria have to be met for there to be moral bonds within both families and political communities (Dworkin 1986; Horton 1992; Hardimon 1994; Mason 1997; Seglow 2013; Lazar 2016). Some suggest that we look at the *generic good* that a community provides in order to determine the moral criteria a community has to meet to give rise to moral bonds. In the case of political communities, Horton argues that this good is the provision of peace, security, and law and order (1992: 162, 176–7). If that is so, the moral criteria a political community has to meet to give rise to moral bonds are rather modest (1992: 160, 163, 178). Ronald Dworkin argues that a "true community" (not only a true political community, but a true community of any kind) must meet a couple of moral criteria, and one of them is that a group's practices display an equal general concern for the well-being of all members (1986: 200–1). Moral bonds including relations of authority can only be found in such true communities. Dworkin's account has the reputation of setting quite ambitious criteria for a proper community, but it should be noted that the criteria do not require perfect justice. There can be legitimate authority and moral bonds in moderately unjust communities (1986: 203–5). Andrew Mason grounds political obligations in the intrinsic value of equal citizenship and the recognition it provides (1997: 439–45). When a polity does not realize equal citizenship, then there are no moral bonds and no legitimate authority.

For our purposes, it does not matter what moral criteria one should adopt, in the end. In any case, introducing such moral criteria is not an ad hoc move. All theories of political authority have to invoke external moral criteria at some point, including consent theory (Horton 1992: 161; Hardimon 1994: 344): Consent theory has to specify under which circumstances consent ceases to be valid, and it has to discuss whether there are things that we cannot give valid consent to (slavery may be such a thing).

Some suspect that once moral criteria are introduced, membership alone is no longer sufficient for the existence of obligations and authority. Richard Dagger writes: "Something extra must be added – an appeal to justice or to the nature of true community – to supply what a straightforward appeal to membership lacks" (2000: 110; see Simmons 1996a: 87–90; Wellman 1997: 199). I do not see much of a problem here (see also Horton and Windeknecht 2015: 912–14). Indeed an advocate of a community-based argument for authority should say that membership in a community alone is not sufficient for having obligations and for authority relations. The community must also meet certain moral standards and, at least sometimes, one also has to self-identify as a member. This does not undermine a community-based argument for authority. The core of a community-based argument for authority is not the claim that membership in a community is sufficient for standing in authority relations to other members. The core of a community-based argument for authority is that we do not need any *grounding* of authority relations. A community-based argument tries to convince us that we can take it as an established, fixed point that certain kinds of communities come with moral bonds including relations of authority. That certain kinds of communities do not come with such moral bonds does not undermine this idea.

A second worry about a community-based argument for political authority is that there are important differences between families and political communities (Simmons 1996a: 91–2; Wellman 1997: 188–9; Dagger 2000: 107–8; Jeske 2001). One of the most obvious differences is that political communities are quite anonymous, while families are not.

We do not know most of our fellow compatriots, but we do know our family, at least that part of our family where we feel that moral bonds exist. Another important difference is that there usually are emotional bonds between family members; in the case of political communities, people may be emotionally attached to their community in the abstract, but they are not emotionally connected with each member. Finally, the emotional bonds within families seem to be *natural* in a deep sense; at least the emotional bonds between parents and children and between siblings are built into our "biological blueprint," so to speak. Political communities, on the other hand, are cultural artifacts and so our attachment to them cannot be as deeply embedded in our human nature.

How should a defender of a community-based argument for political authority reply to this? First, she could try to explain how and why these differences are matters of degree: We do not know *all* family members we are said to have moral bonds with, we do not have strong emotional bonds with all family members (for example to an uncle one rarely meets or one simply does not like), and the tendency to get emotionally attached to groups has deep evolutionary roots, too (Haidt 2012). After all, there is something to Aristotle's famous dictum that "man is by nature a political animal" (2013: Bk 1). Second, the defender could deny the relevance of these (gradual) differences. Sure, there are these differences, but why should they demonstrate that political authority cannot be conceived analogously to parental authority, i.e. as a basic feature of the moral landscape without any need for a deeper explanation? Both replies are good, as far as they go, although one may indeed become a little less confident in the adequacy of the analogy. If you think that there are moral bonds within families *because* there are (in general) emotional ties and a natural affection among members, then you will become suspicious about moral bonds in political communities. But, as I said, a defender of a community-based argument for political authority and moral bonds in political communities need not believe that there are moral bonds *only if and because* there are such natural emotional ties. The core conviction is that we need no deeper explanation about moral bonds in families and political communities because we are so certain about them.

Relatedly, it has been argued that a community-based argument for *political* authority gives a problematically paternalist picture of the state (Dagger 2000: 108). If state authority is taken as similar to parental authority, does this imply that the state should educate us like our parents did? Should the state treat its citizens like children? In reply, one could make the case that – in a sense – of course the state should be for the good of its citizen and in that sense parents may indeed be a proper model (Rousseau 1762: Bk 1 Ch. 2). Moreover, one could point out that this need not imply that the state should treat citizens like children. A proponent of a community-based argument for political authority need not deny that citizens should be conceived as autonomous beings and that this sets limits to what states may legitimately do. To draw an analogy between parental authority and political authority does not commit us to follow it through in every respect.

The third worry is that the community-based argument for political authority confuses *felt* obligations with real obligations (Simmons 1996a: 75, 83; see Dagger 2000: 108–10); likewise, it confuses most people's *de facto* acknowledgment of political authority with *legitimate* authority. Just citing people's conviction that states have political authority is simply not sufficient to show that they actually have political authority. In reply, one can insist that – just like in the case of parental authority – we should take people's intuitions at face value, at least as long as there is no reason for doubt. Ethics and political philosophy have to start somewhere, and where else should we start if not with our firmly held convictions.

But now the objector can respond that indeed there are good reasons to doubt that there are moral bonds and authority relations in political communities. Christopher Wellman describes a cosmopolitan who feels no special connection to his compatriots and cares for people far abroad as much as he does for people at home. Wellman suggests that this person looks not morally depraved, but indeed superior and admirable (1997: 184–5). This is different from the case of someone who does not feel connected to her mother and father or to her children. Maybe, then, the moral bonds in political communities including authority relations turn out to be a mere prejudice that should be overcome?

A second reason to doubt that there are legitimate relations of authority in political communities is that they constitute relations of inequality (see pp. 13–14). Most people adhere to the powerful idea that all humans are equals; and even though the idea of equality can certainly be interpreted in different ways, political authority plainly introduces massive inequality in the moral rights people have. Some are said to have the moral power to impose duties on others and the liberty to enforce them. Some are said to have the right to rule. This is an inequality in the most straightforward sense. It is true that the right to rule basically resides in political institutions, but it is also true that in the end real persons have to fill the institutional roles and therefore have the right to rule. Note that the inequality between parents and children looks much less problematic, since children are not yet fully rational humans. They *are* unequal in the relevant sense. Thus political authority (and moral bonds in political community in general) looks morally problematic in a way that parental authority (and moral bonds in families) does not.

Moreover, we know about people's willingness to accept illegitimate de facto authorities and should therefore be reluctant to treat people's acceptance of state authority as clear evidence that the state actually has legitimate political authority (see Huemer 2013: Ch. 6). The Milgram experiments (see Milgram 1974) showed a surprising willingness in people to submit to immoral directives from authorities, and the so-called Stockholm syndrome describes how victims sometimes tend to build emotional ties with their captors or abusers.

Thus political authority is in need of a deeper explanation, while parental authority is not, or at least not to the same degree. The strategy of just relying on our conviction that there are moral bonds in political communities including relations of authority is in the end unconvincing; one cannot circumvent the *explanation condition* when it comes to political authority.

Now friends of a community-based argument for political authority could of course try to change their strategy and try to *actually provide* a deeper explanation for how moral bonds including relations of authority are brought about in communities. A tempting way is to push the community-based argument in the direction of consent theory (Gilbert 2006; Horton 2012; Renzo 2012; see also Raz 1984: 353–4). When we self-identify with a community, is not our membership consensual, in a way? Couldn't this explain why we are morally connected to the community? Of course, membership is usually not consensual in the sense discussed in Chapter 2, but we might try to attenuate the concept of consent a little bit. Maybe it is not literally consent that is required to establish political authority and, more generally, authority in communities that are not strictly voluntary. Maybe something similar, but weaker, is sufficient, like citizens' *acceptance* of the state or their membership in a community (Horton 2012; Renzo 2012; see also Murphy 1999). Horton emphasizes that acceptance does not itself "ground" legitimacy, though. He writes:

> I consent to, or more properly recognize or acknowledge, the state as legitimate, because it meets the salient criteria of legitimacy that are practically operative. I do not acknowledge its legitimacy because I have consented to it [...]. The affirmation of legitimacy matters, but that affirmation is grounded in something other than that affirmation itself. (2012: 142; see Horton and Windeknecht 2015: 909)

Nevertheless, acceptance seems to be necessary for legitimate authority, according to him.

Acceptance certainly looks similar to consent, at first sight. When people accept the state, they have some kind of positive attitude toward the state; when they give consent to the state, they express that attitude. But consent and acceptance are very different in their moral powers (Wendt 2016b: 237–40). Consent can only do its job of creating rights because it is not a mere mental act or mental state, but some kind of public performance, observable and understandable by others. This is especially clear in the context of consent to sex. My mental acts cannot give some other person the liberty-right to have sexual intercourse with me. For that reason, acceptance is very different from consent. Acceptance is a mental state, not a performance or public act. And as such it cannot create new rights. But a theory of authority must *explain* how the state could come to have rights that the governed lack. Acceptance cannot help with that task; only proper consent can.

Now one may reply that acceptance is not only a mental act, but also behaviorally manifest. One can *observe* that others accept the state, for example in how they talk about it. But either behaviorally manifest acceptance is said to amount to tacit consent, in which case we are back to consent theory, or behaviorally manifest acceptance does not amount to tacit consent, in which case we still lack an explanation of how this acceptance could give rise to new rights for some persons.

A fourth and final worry about community-based accounts is that they probably fail to meet the *success condition*. At least when subjective endorsement of membership plays an important role, not every citizen will incur political obligations and be subject to political authority. Some punks, anarchists, and stubborn cosmopolitans will not be members in the relevant sense. This may be not so problematic when we merely aim to explain political obligations. One can concede that the account cannot explain *everyone's* political obligations, when it succeeds in explaining the political obligations of most or many citizens. But for an account of political authority, the fact that some are not members in the relevant sense is problematic, since states as we know them claim to have authority over *all* citizens and people who are in their territory (that is what I called the holistic nature of political authority; see p. 7). Political authority is not individualized, such that a state could have authority over some citizens, but not over others. Hence political authority in the full sense does not exist in any actual and imaginable future state, when we subscribe to a community-based argument for political authority (see also van der Vossen 2011: 493–4).

Summary

If we take moral bonds within political communities as analogous to moral bonds within families, we can try to circumvent the *explanation condition* and simply treat political authority as a basic fact that is not in need of any deeper explanation. The problem is that the analogy between families and political communities does not hold insofar as there are good reasons to doubt that there are moral bonds within political communities and that states have political authority. For that reason, we need some explanation for political authority and cannot circumvent the *explanation condition*. Moreover, the community-based account cannot account for the holistic nature of political authority.

5
Natural Duties and Authority

Some have tried to ground political authority in our natural duties. Natural duties are nothing obscure; they are simply moral duties we all have as humans, i.e. independently of our specific roles as mothers or teachers and independently of our promises and contracts. I will discuss three natural duty-based theories. The first works with a natural duty of justice. The second does so as well, but claims to be able to explain not only the authority of the state, but also the specific authority of democracy. The third works with a natural duty to rescue others in emergency situations.

The natural duty of justice

At first blush, one might think that the connection between authority and justice should be very simple. When states do a reasonably good job of securing and promoting justice, then they have political authority for that very reason. Justice is a big word, of course. I would like to stay agnostic on the details of the requirements of justice. Justice will probably require that certain basic liberal rights (the right to physical integrity, freedom of speech, religious freedom, and so on) are protected, that resources and opportunities are fairly distributed in the society, that criminals are caught and punished, etc. Justice is often conceived as the main virtue of social institutions, and so one might well be inclined to think that states that help to secure or promote justice thereby acquire political authority. But this line of thought would be a bit too simple. There are other institutions beyond the state that also help to secure and promote justice, and we are not willing to grant them political authority. Oxfam or Amnesty International, for example, may advance the cause of justice, but they do not have the authority to impose and coercively enforce laws on us. In fact, they do not have the moral power to impose any duties on us. For that reason, the connection between justice and authority is a bit more complicated. The simple fact that an institution helps with the cause of justice is not sufficient to bring political authority into the world.

A promising way to find a bridge from a state's justice to its authority is to appeal to people's "natural duties of justice." As explained, natural duties are duties one has simply as a human being, i.e. independently of community- or consent-based obligations. An example of a natural duty is our duty not to kill others. Some think that there also is a natural duty of justice "to support and to further just institutions." According to John Rawls, our natural duty of justice has two parts: "[F]irst, we are to comply with and to do our share in just institutions when they exist and apply to us; and second, we are to assist in the establishment of just arrangements when they do not exist, at least when this can be done with little cost to ourselves" (1971: 334, and see 115). What is of interest for us is the first part, the duty to comply with and do our share in existing just institutions that apply to us. That we have such a duty sounds quite plausible; and if we do, then this is an important first step in an argument for political authority: We have a natural duty to comply with and do our share in just institutions including just *states*. This arguably means, in the context of states, that we have a duty to obey the laws, pay taxes, maybe to serve in the military, etc.

That we have such a duty is not sufficient to show that political institutions have authority. But when we add the assumption that we do not have "a right not to be coerced to do what we have an obligation of justice to do" (Buchanan 2002: 703), then we already have an argument why just states at least have a liberty-right to enact and coercively enforce laws. Before we take the second step from here to the state's power to impose duties (and hence to political authority), I would like to add a couple of comments and discuss two objections to the argument so far.

Recall the *target condition* (p. 15): It is nice if an account of political authority can also explain other forms of authority. But if it cannot, it should be able to explain why. The natural duty of justice is only invoked to explain state authority. Why does it not apply to theoretical authorities, to parental authority, and to the authority of bosses, religious leaders, and teachers? One may argue that only states have the job of securing and promoting justice. Parents, for example, have the job of promoting the well-being of their children, first of all, but not of promoting justice. Yet all authorities can influence the justice of a society, and all authorities arguably owe certain duties of justice to their subjects. To meet the *target condition*, it would therefore be worthwhile to try to develop natural duty-based accounts of parental authority, the authority of bosses, the authority of religious leaders, and even theoretical authorities. Nevertheless, I will here focus on political authority only.

If the natural duty of justice account succeeds, it seems that it will probably have no problem in accounting for the holistic nature of political authority (see p. 7), and this certainly is a great attraction. Because we *all* have natural duties of justice, no matter if we like it or not, the account promises to explain the state's authority over all of us. There is no way for some people to escape state authority (as long as states are just, of course). The theory thus promises to meet the *success condition*.

A natural duty of justice-based account of political authority has roots in Immanuel Kant. As explained in Chapter 2, Kant argues that we have a natural duty to leave the state of nature in order to achieve equal freedom under the rule of law (1793: Sec. 2; 1797: Part I §42).

Two objections

There are two objections to the story so far. The first objection is that it is not of much interest whether we have a duty to comply with and do our share in *just states*, since no actual states are truly just, and none will ever be. Whether we have a duty to comply with just states is of purely academic interest, a special issue in highly unrealistic utopian political philosophy (see Horton 1992: 103–5). Moreover, there is disagreement about what justice requires precisely; how could we ever know that we live in a just state?

This objection is important, but the easy answer is to concede its point and downgrade the natural duty of justice a little bit. Jonathan Quong argues convincingly that the natural duty to comply and do one's share in just institutions does not only apply to perfectly just institutions. Because there is reasonable disagreement about justice, the natural duty of justice already applies when institutions are "reasonably just" (2011: 132–5). There may still be some vagueness in the idea that institutions are to be "reasonably just," but this seems unavoidable. In any case, the natural duty of justice is supposed to apply under realistic, non-utopian conditions. In a similar spirit, Allen Buchanan proposes a natural duty of justice "to help ensure that all persons have access to institutions that protect their basic human rights." That duty applies as soon as states do a "credible job of protecting at least the most basic human rights of all those over whom it wields power" (2002: 703). Doing a credible job of protecting the most basic human rights is certainly not utopian, and it is a fundamental advancement of justice when this job is done.

The second objection is that the natural duty of justice cannot explain why we are bound to *particular* states, i.e. why a citizen of Ghana is bound to the Ghanaian state, while a citizen of France is bound to the state of France (presupposing, of course, that both Ghana and France are reasonably just states). Why is a Mexican citizen supposed to pay taxes in Mexico and not elsewhere? Why should a citizen of Vietnam do his military service in Vietnam and not elsewhere? How, in general, can the natural duty of justice explain special ties with one's country? This, in short, is the *particularity objection* (Simmons 1979: 147–56; 2005: 162–79).

The *particularity objection* does not apply to consent-based or community-based accounts. When political authority is grounded in consent, it is clear why I am bound to a particular state – because I consented to *that* state's authority. When political authority is grounded in community, it is also clear why I am bound to a particular state – because I am a member in *that* political community. But a natural duty of justice-based account cannot explain why people are bound to particular states, since there are many reasonably just institutions in the world and I could do my share in all of them. When we start with a universal natural duty of justice, we cannot end up with particularized duties to particular states, just because the very point of natural duties is that they apply independently of special roles or acts of consent that could constitute particularist connections.

If a natural duty of justice-based account cannot answer the *particularity objection*, it will also have a hard time accounting for political authority (in a second step). If there are no particularized bonds between individuals and states, one can hardly explain why states have legitimate authority over their citizens and everyone in their territory, but not over other people.

Now one may think that there is an easy answer to the *particularity objection*. According to the natural duty of justice-based account, we have moral bonds with the institutions that *apply to us*. That is how Rawls formulates the duty. But what does it mean that a political institution "applies" to someone? John Simmons presents the example of the (fictional) Institute for the Advancement of Philosophers in Montana. Let us assume that the Institute pursues a just cause and that it "applies" to me, since I am a philosopher. Do I have a duty to support the Institute in one way or another? It does not seem so: "People cannot simply force institutions on me, no matter how just, and force on me a moral bond to do my part in and comply with those institutions" (1979: 148). Of course, things change once I actively become a member, but then the reason for the moral bonds is not a natural duty of justice, but my consent. Mere "application" cannot be the point, says Simmons.

One reply by defenders of a natural duty of justice-based account is to simply drop the idea of particularized moral bonds between states and citizens and to endorse a globalist, transnational duty to support just institutions (see Rinderle 2005: 261–3). But since a state's *political authority* certainly is not global and transnational, but specific to a state's citizens and territory, this reply will not help if we would like to ground political authority (in a second step).

A better answer to the *particularity objection* is to claim that some institutions – namely states – are *necessary* for establishing justice and, second, that they require territorial jurisdiction in order to be able to establish justice (Waldron 1993; Quong 2011: 129–30). To establish institutions that protect people's basic liberal rights and try to achieve a fair distribution of resources and opportunities among citizens arguably requires territorial states. The states we live in are the ones we have to comply with because they apply to us *qua* territorial states. In that they differ from Simmons's Institute for the Advancement of Philosophers in Montana. In the end, then, institutions can indeed "impose" themselves on us (Waldron 1993: 27–30; Christiano 2004: 281–3).

Some may still be skeptical about this answer to the *particularity objection*. First of all, anarchists could of course question the necessity of the territorial state to establish justice. This is less of a philosophical doubt, of course, but I will briefly deal with it in Chapter 7.

A second problem is the moral arbitrariness of territorial borders (Simmons 2005: 173–4). If the territoriality of states is to particularize our duties of justice, then the actual territorial borders of states should better not be morally arbitrary or – even worse – based on a history of conquest and war. But a defender of a natural duty of justice-based account may insist that the justice of territorial borders is beside the point. Territorial states are needed for establishing justice, and when they are (now) reasonably just, we have to support the states we live in, no matter whether their borders are morally arbitrary. They are now morally salient, and so we have to work with them.

Third, one might worry that the *particularity objection* has still not been *fully* answered. That states are necessary for establishing justice and require territorial jurisdiction in order to be able to establish justice may explain particularized bonds between states and *everyone in their territory*. But it cannot explain why there should be any bonds between states and citizens who live abroad or visit some other country for a limited period of time. Conversely, it cannot explain why tourists and foreign residents in a state's territory are not bound to that state in the same way that citizens are (Mason 1997: 437).

But maybe proponents of a natural duty-based account need not worry too much about answering *that* version of the *particularity objection*. Maybe they can simply endorse the view that there are no natural duty-based bonds between expats and their home states, and that citizens, tourists, and foreign residents all have the same natural duty-based bonds with the territorial state they happen to be in. This would obviously change the scope of the state's liberty-right to enact and enforce laws: States could no longer be said to have that liberty-right with regard to expat citizens, and tourists would be beyond the reach of their home states while abroad. It would also change the scope of the state's power to impose duties (if a natural duty-based account can explain that power in a second step): States could no longer be said to have that power with regard to citizens who are not in their home state's territory. This would mean rethinking the holistic nature of political authority. A state's authority would still be holistic with regard to its territory, but not with regard to its citizens. That may be a bullet one can bite. But maybe one need not even bite that bullet: To account for the special ties of citizenship, proponents of a natural duty-based account might try to combine it with a community-based account (see Mokrosinska 2012: Ch. 7; Schmelzle 2015: 119–23) (see also pp. 91, 100).

From natural duties of justice to political authority

Let us assume that we have established that people have a natural duty of justice to comply with a particular (reasonably just) state and that reasonably just states have the liberty-right to enact and enforce laws for a certain territory. Some proponents of a natural duty of justice-based account, like Rawls and Buchanan, stop at this point. But others aim to take a second step and to base the state's *authority* on a natural duty of justice (Quong 2011: 108, 128). We thus have to show how reasonably just states could acquire the moral power to impose duties on citizens.

One option would be to follow Elizabeth Anscombe when she writes: "If something is necessary, if it is, for example, a necessary task in human life, then a right arises in those whose task it is, to have what belongs to the performance of the task" (1978: 17; see Sartorius 1981; Copp 1999). Because states are necessary for establishing justice and because they need political authority to do so, they have political authority. But this is unconvincing (see also Simmons 2005: 127–42), since it is simply a refusal to provide an explanation for political authority (which is problematic, as pointed out in the last chapter). Something more needs to be said, and the most promising way is to draw a connection between authority and the natural duty of justice again.

Quong proposes a principle that applies not only to political authority, but also to "local" authorities like that of the flight attendant in Estlund's example from Chapter 2 (pp. 31–2). Quong writes:

> One way to establish that a person has legitimate authority over another person involves showing that the alleged subject is likely better to fulfil the duties of justice he is under if he accepts the directives of the alleged authority as authoritatively binding and tries to follow them, rather than by trying to directly fulfil the duties he is under himself. (2011: 128)

The principle obviously resembles Joseph Raz's *normal justification thesis* (see p. 45), but it works with natural duties of justice instead of reasons. Quong presents the following example (2011: 127): Two persons, A and B, arrive at the scene of an accident. A has medical expertise, B has not. Quong suggests that, under these circumstances, B has a moral duty to follow A's directives, because this is the best way for her to fulfil her moral duty to help the victims, which is a natural moral duty. A thus acquires authority over B because B has a natural duty to help the victims.

In the example, A indeed seems to have acquired a moral power to impose duties. But it is weaker than a typical moral power to impose duties (see also Wendt 2016a: 117–21). First of all, it is a power that is constrained in many ways. It only applies under the present exceptional circumstances for a short period of time and for a narrow set of permissible directives that all have to do with helping the victims of the accident. Some may want to call it mere "leadership," not authority (see p. 32). Second, it is merely a power to specify pre-existing duties. A power to specify a pre-existing duty is not exactly the same as a mere side-effect power (see pp. 10–11). It indeed is a power to provide content-independent reasons for action. But it is also not a power to impose duties in its fullest sense, because it is not a power to impose new duties, but only to specify a pre-existing duty.

Can we understand political authority by analogy with Quong's example? Of course one might worry that it cannot establish a proper power to impose duties, merely a power to specify a pre-existing duty. But maybe one should not worry too much about this. A moral power to specify a pre-existing duty of justice might be all we need.

It is a bigger problem that the authority (or leadership) of the doctor and the authority of the state are so different in their comprehensiveness. The accident example is so convincing because there is a clear task (one has to help the victims), clear expertise (the doctor knows how to help, I do not), and clear limits to authority (once the task is done, authority ends). All these factors are different in the case of political authority. There is no clearly specified task, no clear expertise, and no clear limits to authority. Political authority implies a very general power to impose duties on all matters, and it is hard to see how this can be understood as necessary for giving direction to a pre-existing duty of justice.

Another problem is that private companies or NGOs may also be in a great position to specify my natural duty of justice. Why do they not acquire the same authority as the state? It seems that a natural duty of justice-based account cannot convincingly explain the authority of states and thus does not meet the *explanation condition*.

Democracy and authority

I now come to the second natural duty-based account. It aims at explaining not only state authority, but also the specific authority of democracy. Most people believe that democracies are morally superior to other types of state. Some think so for instrumental and pragmatic reasons (recall Winston Churchill saying "democracy is the worst form of government except for all those other forms that have been tried from time to time"); others think that democracies are intrinsically valuable for reasons that have to do with self-rule, freedom, and/or equality. Some argue that there also is a pretty direct link between democracy and political authority. They are inspired by, among others, Jean-Jacques Rousseau. Rousseau provides a social contract argument for state authority and argues that the only legitimate contract is one that establishes a (direct) democracy (1762: Bk. 1 Chs. 6–7, Bk. 2 Chs. 1–2).

Among contemporary philosophers, Thomas Christiano has provided one of the best-known arguments for why states have political authority *and* have to be democratic (2004; 2008). Christiano starts with a principle of justice and then goes on to argue that democracies are "uniquely suited" to advancing that principle (2004: 269–77; 2008: Chs. 1–3). The principle of justice is called the *principle of the public realization of equal advancement of interests*. What matters most, in our context, is that it takes justice to require publicity. Justice not only has to be done, it has to be seen to be done. The background for the need for publicity is our fallibility in thinking about justice and our disagreement about justice. Under these conditions, everyone has an interest in being able to see that she is treated as an equal and thus able to "feel at home." Christiano thinks that democracy is uniquely suited for advancing the *principle of the public realization of equal advancement of interests*, because it gives everyone an equal say in political decisions and in that sense respects everyone's judgment (see also Waldron 1999: 113–16). Of course, democracy is not the only institutional means for the *principle of the equal advancement of interests*; basic liberal rights like freedom of speech and freedom of association have the same source.

Now what has all this to do with authority? Christiano claims, first of all, that the state is necessary to establish justice (2004: 281–3). Like Kant, he believes that justice is impossible without states. For that reason, he endorses the principle that "if legislative institutions publicly realize justice, then they have legitimate legislative authority over those people within their jurisdiction" (2004: 285). If that principle is convincing, it is plausible that only democratic states can have political authority, because only democratic states publicly realize justice *in themselves*, i.e. not due to the justice of the outcomes they produce, but simply because they are democratic. It should be noted that the authority of democracy is limited by the substantive justice of the democratic decisions, according to Christiano: Democratic decisions must not publicly violate justice by infringing liberal rights (2004: 287–90; 2008: Ch. 7). But when we put this caveat to the side, then Christiano's basic argument is that (1) only democracies are just, (2) just states have political authority, and (3) hence only democracies have political authority.

Now of course one may well question Christiano's starting point, the *principle of the public realization of equal advancement of interests*, and one can also raise doubts whether that principle really requires democracy (Wall 2006; Huemer 2013: 68–77; Viehoff 2014: 348–51). But the key step in Christiano's argument for political authority is the claim that states which publicly realize justice have political authority simply because they are necessary for establishing justice. Is not political authority established by mere say-so here? Why exactly do states that publicly realize justice thereby gain political authority? As long as there is no answer to this, the *explanation condition* is not satisfied.

Yet Christiano indeed provides the missing link. It is, again, a natural duty of justice. He writes: "The state is engaged in an activity that is a morally necessary one in the sense that someone who fails to comply with the state's publicly promulgated rules is merely violating a duty of justice to his fellow citizens" (2004: 283). In general terms, everyone has a natural duty of justice "to treat other human beings as equals and this implies that each person must try to realize the equal advancement of the interests of other human beings" (2008: 249). Accordingly, citizens have a duty to comply with democratic states because this is required by their duty of justice.

Now we can see that Christiano's argument has a similar basis to Rawls's. As such, it faces the same challenges, too.

One is to answer the *particularity objection*. Christiano writes:

> Notice that each has a duty to comply with their own democratic institutions since these institutions are necessary to treating their fellows publicly as equals. The duty to treat people as equals is not fully discharged by trying to support the construction of democracy in other parts of the world. If one only did this and failed to act in accordance with a reasonably well-constituted democratic order, then one would be treating one's fellows publicly as inferiors. And this would be a very weighty violation of equality. (2008: 250)

This may again not *fully* answer the *particularity objection*, since it is not sufficient to explain why one has special moral ties with one's home country even when living abroad (see p. 73), but – again – this may be a bullet one can bite.

The other problem is to find a bridge from the natural duty of justice to the state's power to impose duties. As we saw in our discussion of Quong, this is rather difficult. Political authority looks too all-encompassing to be understood by analogy with the authority (or leadership) of a doctor at the scene of a car accident who specifies people's natural duty to help the victims. As long as there is no better explanation, the *explanation condition* is not met.

There are philosophers who have proposed alternative arguments for a close connection between equality and democratic authority or between equal freedom and democratic authority (Buchanan 2002; Marmor 2005; Stilz 2009; Kolodny 2014; Viehoff 2014). I cannot discuss their views here. I believe that the difficulty of bridging the gap between people's natural duties and the state's moral power to impose duties will affect all these attempts as well.

As a side-note: It seems to me that most discussions of "democratic legitimacy" (see e.g. Cohen 1989; Habermas 1992; Peter 2008) are not really about political authority, understood as the state's right to rule, but about how political decisions ought to be made. Other debates about democracy are simply about what is good and bad about democracies and whether democracy has not only instrumental, but also intrinsic value (as those who see democracies as closely related to values like equality and freedom tend to think). I think that all these debates are situated at a lower level than debates about political authority. They *presuppose* that states can have political authority, under certain conditions, and ask what institutional form states should take (and why).

Likewise, to show that only democracies are publicly justifiable (Lefkowitz 2005; Estlund 2008) is not to show that democratic states have political authority. The public justifiability of democracy means, roughly, that everyone has sufficient reason to accept it, or at least that no one can reasonably reject it. Public justifiability can be translated into the language of hypothetical consent: If democracy is publicly justifiable, then everyone will *agree* to endorse democracy (under appropriate circumstances). I think that the public justifiability of democracy could at best show that democracies are superior to other state forms, and that we have good reasons to support democracies, but it cannot establish the political authority of democratic states, for reasons spelled out in Chapter 2.

Samaritanism and authority

A third natural duty-based argument has been devised by Christopher Wellman. Wellman does not invoke natural duties of justice, but what he calls "samaritan duties." Samaritan duties are basically natural duties to rescue others in emergency situations. For example, Wellman presents the case of Antonio picking up a hitchhiker who wants to go to a nearby town called Pleasantville. Once they get there, it turns out that Pleasantville is not pleasant at all, but a "contemporary Hobbesian state of nature." In that scenario, Antonio quite plausibly has a moral duty to bring the hitchhiker to safety; he may not leave her in Pleasantville (1996: 214). More generally, says Wellman, we have a duty to save others from peril when we can do so without unreasonable costs for ourselves and our help is indeed necessary (1996: 215; 2001: 744). This duty should indeed be rather uncontroversial.

Now what he calls "state legitimacy" – the liberty-right of the state to enact and coercively enforce laws – can be understood as based on people's samaritan duties, says Wellman. How does that work? Well, the state is necessary to establish peace, security, and law and order; without the police, military, and courts, we would have civil war and instability, basically like the Hobbesian state of nature. Because this is so, we have a samaritan duty to save all of us from the perils of the Hobbesian state of nature by allowing the state to do its job of establishing peace, security, and law and order. This establishes the state's liberty-right to enact and enforce laws. Like Antonio is not at liberty to leave the hitchhiker in Pleasantville, we are not at liberty to be free from laws and state coercion, because the territorial state saves us from the Hobbesian state of nature (1996: 216–19, 223; 2001: 745–7; 2005: 23). With its focus on peace, Wellman's theory is the natural duty account that is closest to Thomas Hobbes.

So far we have seen a samaritan duty-based defense of the state's liberty-right to enact and enforce (certain kinds of) laws. But, says Wellman, we have not yet established a general duty to obey on the part of the citizens, simply because it is not the case that every citizen's compliance is necessary for the state to be able to deliver its benefits: "The plain truth is that any given citizen's behavior typically has no discernible effect on her state's capacity to perform its functions" (2001: 749). But Wellman goes on to argue that everyone has to do his or her *fair share* in the societal rescuing enterprise, and that this means that everyone has a general duty to obey the law (2001: 749–51; 2005: 32–3).

Wellman's theory aims to overcome the *particularity objection* in a distinctive way. Duties of rescue are individuated by the facts of the emergency situation. If I pass by a pond and see a drowning child, it is me and not someone else who has the duty to rescue that child. Likewise, my political community is the pond in which the other members and I are all about to drown, and so I and not foreigners have a duty to rescue the members of my community. More precisely, Wellman argues that it would be unfair to claim discretion in *how* to discharge one's samaritan duty; one has to comply with the laws of one's own state, since wide conformity with the laws of a state is necessary to solve the problem territorial states are to solve (2005: 37–45). That is why I am particularly bound to my state.

But there are several worries about his argument (besides the obvious anarchist objection that the state is not necessary to achieve peace; see Chapter 7). First, like other natural duty-based accounts (see pp. 73, 78), Wellman's attempt to overcome the *particularity objection* does not *fully* solve the problem. It cannot explain why there should be bonds between a state and expat citizens who do not live in its territory (Renzo 2008). Wellman simply concedes this and bites the bullet (2005: 46–52).

Second, one may doubt that the Hobbesian state of nature is an actual danger lurking in the background of our daily lives (Knowles 2010: 164–5). Most people never think about it at all, and, even on reflection, it does not look like an immediate threat, an emergency, or something we have to be saved from here and now, at least in countries that are not actually facing a civil war.

Third, it can be quite costly to comply with the state. One may have to go into the military, one has to pay taxes, etc. Since samaritan duties only apply when there are no "unreasonable costs" to bear, they can arguably not ground a very robust duty to obey (Klosko 2005: 93–4; Simmons 2005: 181–2). The obvious reply is that indeed compliance with the state may sometimes be costly, but not unreasonably costly, given the benefits the state provides (Wellman 2001: 746; 2005: 32). But, as a rejoinder, one can well insist that individual compliance is simply not necessary to achieve peace, security, and law and order, and in light of this fact the costs may indeed *be* "unreasonable." If that is right, the samaritan argument is undermined.

Fourth, and most importantly, Wellman does not attempt to take the second step from people's natural duties and the state's liberty-right to enact and enforce laws to the state's power to impose duties (i.e. political authority). The theory thus does not fare better in explaining political authority than other natural duty-based theories, and for that reason it does not satisfy the *explanation condition*.

Summary

I have discussed three theories that try to ground political authority in our natural duties. The first two start with a natural duty of justice; what is specific about the second is that it tries to establish the specific authority of democracy as well. The third starts not with a natural duty of justice, but with a natural duty of rescue. There are two main problems for all natural duty-based accounts. One is to answer the *particularity objection*; the other is to explain the step from people's natural duties to the state's power to impose duties on them.

6
Fair Cooperation and Authority

Most people agree that the state does not have the consent of the greatest part of the citizenry. But maybe there are other ways to voluntarily incur obligations and establish relations of authority. The most prominent candidate is fairness obligations. When people voluntarily accept benefits that are produced cooperatively, then they arguably have an obligation of fairness to do their part in the cooperative scheme that produces these benefits. If the state could be conceived as part of such a cooperative venture, maybe people have a fairness obligation to comply with its laws and do their share, and maybe one can also understand the state's authority as based on fairness considerations. Like consent theory, this account has roots in Plato's *Crito*.

The principle of fairness

Consider the inhabitants of a rural village who suffer from yearly droughts and understand that they would all be better off with a dam. Building the dam, though, requires contributions from everyone, in terms of both money and time. Now the fairness principle says that each of the farmers has an obligation to do his or her share in building the dam. Since everyone would benefit from the dam, it would be unfair to free ride on the efforts of the others and take the benefits of the dam without contributing to its construction.

The principle of fairness has been devised by H. L. A. Hart (1955) and John Rawls (1964). Here is Hart's version: "[W]hen a number of persons conduct any joint enterprise according to rules and thus restrict their liberty, those who have submitted to these restrictions when required have a right to a similar submission from those who have benefited by their submission" (1955: 185). So the main thought is that when there is a joint enterprise that requires some sacrifice, those who benefit from it have an obligation to do their part in the enterprise.

Robert Nozick has famously criticized the fairness principle. He provides several stories that are supposed to be counterexamples or at least to point to difficulties with the principle. In one of these stories people establish a local radio station in your neighborhood and alternate in presenting an entertainment program for the others (1974: 93–4). In the first week Tim reads his latest poems, in the second week Linda plays guitar and sings folk songs, in the third week George tells a couple of jokes. There is an expectation that every neighbor presents something sooner or later. Maybe there even is a list on which every neighbor has a date assigned at which he or she is to do a show. You usually tune in and actually enjoy what you hear – but do you have an obligation to come up with an entertainment program yourself? According to the fairness principle, the answer seems to be "yes." There is a cooperative venture and you benefit from it, so you have to do your part in it.

But things are a little bit more complicated. For one thing, whether you incur an obligation certainly depends on whether the benefits outweigh the costs for you. If you think that the burden of running a show yourself outweighs all the benefits the entertainment system brings, then arguably you do not have a fairness obligation to run a show (Nozick 1974: 94; Simmons 1979: 133–6; Klosko 1992: 39, 54–7; Wolff 1995: 96). Relatedly, and more generally, people can only incur a fairness obligation if the burdens and benefits of the cooperative venture are fairly distributed (Simmons 1979:

109–14; Greenawalt 1987: 129–33, 141–4; Klosko 1992: 39, Ch. 3). If you are supposed to run 75 percent of the shows, then you do not have a fairness obligation to do it.

Second, Nozick's story shows that obligations cannot simply be forced on people. In the example, you were never asked and you never agreed to do a radio show. In another of Nozick's examples (1974: 95), someone walks around the neighborhood and puts interesting books in people's mailboxes. (We may assume that the books are the product of some joint enterprise.) Even if the recipients actually read and enjoy the books, they do not seem to have an obligation to pay for the books if the person later rings the bell and demands payment. Here the reason seems to be that the recipients of the books were not even part of a joint enterprise. Plausibly, mere bystanders to a cooperative scheme who happen to benefit from the scheme cannot incur any fairness obligations; only *participants* can (Simmons 1979: 120–3). This is something Hart arguably implies, too, when he speaks about a number of people "conducting a joint enterprise." Yet in the entertainment example, we may be unsure whether you are a participant or a bystander in the relevant sense.

So what does it mean to be a participant in a cooperative scheme? A farmer who tries to free ride on the efforts of others and does not contribute to the construction of the dam should arguably count as a participant, even though he does not do his share. So participation cannot mean actually contributing to the production of the benefits. An obligation to contribute is what participants incur even if they have not contributed so far.

One criterion for participation (in the sense relevant for fairness obligations) could be whether the benefits from the cooperative scheme are *voluntarily accepted* (Rawls 1964: 122; 1971: 111–12; Bell 1978; Simmons 1979: 125–6; 1993: 256–7; Dagger 1997: 70). When people refuse to receive the relevant benefits, then they obviously do not voluntarily accept them. But things are more complicated in the case of non-excludable goods. Clean air is a classic example of a non-excludable good, national defense another. Once they are produced, nobody can be excluded from their consumption. If one cannot refuse to receive the benefits of clean air and national defense, how can one voluntarily accept them in a meaningful sense? Simmons argues that one genuinely accepts a non-excludable good when one consumes it "willingly and knowingly" (1979: 130–2). This means at least that one has to be aware that the benefits are not manna from heaven, but the result of cooperative efforts to which one could contribute. It probably also means that one has to think that the good is worth its price. Therefore, I might indeed have a fairness obligation to contribute in the entertainment system example, if I actually tune in and accept the benefits willingly and knowingly in that sense. In the case where someone throws books in my mailbox, I probably do not. Even if I read the books and enjoy them, I will not think that they are the result of some cooperative enterprise to which I could contribute.

Since benefits have to be voluntarily accepted, the fairness account has close similarities to consent theory. Both ground obligations (and in the end authority) on voluntary acts, in one case consent, in the other acceptance of benefits from cooperation. Voluntary acceptance is not the same as tacit consent. One can voluntarily accept benefits without there being any convention that would count such acceptance as consent; in fact one can voluntarily accept benefits without anyone noticing one's acceptance. This also explains the attraction of the fairness account. Universal consent to the state is not to be had, but universal acceptance of state benefits might look more promising.

So far we have modified the principle of fairness in two respects: When there is a cooperative enterprise that requires some sacrifice from the members, then one incurs a fairness obligation, first, only if one voluntarily accepts the benefits of the cooperative venture, and, second, only if the burdens and benefits are fairly distributed and the benefits are worth the costs.

Now there is a third modification that one should add. If people who do not contribute can simply be excluded, such that they no longer receive the benefits, then arguably no fairness obligations arise for them. After all, in such cases one can achieve fairness without putting someone under a fairness obligation (Klosko 1992: 35). Again this explains why the dam example and the radio entertainment example are more plausible examples of fairness obligations than the book example. It is hard to exclude people from the benefits of a dam or from the consumption of radio entertainment, but one can easily stop throwing books into people's mailboxes.

Peter Rinderle argues that there are fairness obligations even when people can be excluded, because exclusion raises the price for the production of the benefits (2005: 199–206). If everyone contributed, the good could be produced at lesser costs. This is true, but it does not show that it would be fair to morally require everyone to contribute, if there are other means to achieve fairness. There is nothing unfair about bearing the costs for excluding non-cooperators from the consumption of the good.

Does it help with political obligations?

So far, so good. Does the principle of fairness help with political authority? As in the case of natural duties, it is helpful to split the argument into two parts. In a first step, the fairness principle is to establish political obligations; in a second step, we try to get from political obligations to political authority. It should be noted, though, that many proponents of the fairness account stop at political obligations.

So how can the fairness principle help with political obligations? Can it show that people have obligations to obey the law, to pay taxes, and maybe to serve in the military? Recall what we need for fairness obligations to come up: (1) There is a cooperative enterprise that requires some sacrifice from the participants; (2) you voluntarily accept the benefits that are provided through the cooperative enterprise; (3) the burdens and benefits are fairly distributed and the benefits are worth the costs; and (4) you cannot be excluded such that you no longer receive the benefits – in other words, the cooperative enterprise produces a non-excludable good. When all four conditions are met, then you have a fairness obligation to do your part in the cooperative scheme.

The fourth condition is relatively unproblematic. Our societies do produce non-excludable goods, like national defense and law and order. Let us stipulate that there are no problems with the third condition as well. The first condition may look problematic. There just seem to be too many conflicts and too much coercion infused in our societies to let them appear as clear-cut systems of cooperation comparable to the systems of cooperation in our stories of the dam and the radio entertainment system (Simmons 1979: 140; Horton 1992: 90–1). But let us put this worry to the side and assume, for the sake of the argument, that our societies can be understood as systems of cooperation in the relevant sense. The decisive question, then, is whether people voluntarily accept these goods (i.e. whether the second condition is met). If they do, they incur an obligation, and this obligation arguably requires them to pay taxes and to obey the law, since these are means for producing goods like national defense and law and order.

Do most people voluntarily accept those goods? Following Simmons, this would mean that they accept them "willingly and knowingly." But many citizens "barely notice (and seem disinclined to think about) the benefits they receive" (Simmons 1979: 139). Moreover, even if they *are* aware of the benefits they receive, to accept them "willingly and knowingly" arguably implies also being aware of their price and thinking the benefits are worth it. Again, some people will not meet that condition.

> [M]any more, faced with high taxes, with military service which may involve fighting in foreign "police actions," or with unreasonably restrictive laws governing private pleasures, believe that the benefits received from governments are not worth the price they are forced to pay. (Simmons 1979: 139)

If this is so, not all citizens can be conceived as having fairness obligations in our societal cooperative scheme. Therefore, the account cannot explain the holistic nature of political authority (see p. 7). It does not satisfy the *success condition* (see p. 15). Indeed Rawls, the other early proponent of the fairness account besides Hart, later came to think that most people do not actively accept the benefits of cooperation. He concluded that the principle of fairness does not help much with political obligations (1971: 113–14), and moved on to a natural duty-based account for that reason.

Of course, some are more optimistic that we can conceive citizens as voluntarily accepting the benefits of societal cooperation. Some argue that one need not be conscious of societal cooperation as the source of the relevant good in order to voluntarily accept it in the sense that gives rise to fairness obligations (Arneson 1982: 633; Kavka 1986: 411; Greenawalt 1987: 135–6; Gans 1992: 61–3; Dagger 1997: 73–5). Yet Simmons seems right that a fairness concern only comes up when people really try to take a free ride on the efforts of others, and taking a free ride presumes the relevant knowledge and understanding of the situation (2001: 37–42). For that reason, the prospects for showing that the benefits of societal cooperation are voluntarily accepted by all or almost all citizens in a way that gives rise to fairness obligations are rather bleak.

Fairness obligations without voluntary acceptance of benefits?

Some have questioned whether voluntary acceptance really is a necessary condition for fairness obligations at all (Arneson 1982; Kavka 1986: 411; Greenawalt 1987: 127–9; Klosko 1992: 48–54; Wolff 1995: 95–6; Renzo 2014; see also Simmons 2001: 32–3). I will here focus on George Klosko's theory. He argues that the main problem with some of Nozick's examples is not that the benefits are not freely accepted, but that the goods involved are of minor importance. Things look different in the case of what he calls "indispensable goods" (1992: 39–48). Indispensable goods are presumably beneficial to all members of the community; they are necessary for an acceptable life. National defense, law and order, and relief from various forms of pollution and environmental hazards are such goods. Klosko argues that it does not matter whether these goods are voluntarily accepted or actively pursued: "[B]ecause the benefits of national defense are presumptively beneficial, we can presume that [everyone] *would* pursue them (and bear the associated costs) if this were necessary for their receipt" (1992: 41–2). Because the goods mentioned are non-excludable, it is not possible to exclude anyone in order to achieve fairness. It is also not possible to simply not produce these goods, since they are, after all, indispensable. Hence everyone has an obligation to do her part in the enterprise of producing these indispensable goods. This is a promising first step in a fairness-based argument for political authority. I will talk about the second step – from political obligations to political authority – in a minute. But if the first step succeeds, *everyone* can be said to have political obligations, and so we can expect to explain the holistic nature of political authority.

But there are a couple of objections to Klosko's fairness principle. First, the account could (at best) account for obligations to do one's part in the production of indispensable goods like national defense or law and order. It cannot account for an obligation to comply with all the laws that have nothing to do with these indispensable goods (see Beran 1987: 79–81; Greenawalt 1987: 138–40; Carr 2002: 24–5; Huemer 2013: 88–93). This holds, for example, for laws that prohibit the consumption of drugs, laws that prevent harm to animals, and all tax laws that are related to state-run welfare programs. Proponents of the fairness principle reply that it might be possible to extend the function of cooperative schemes that already produce indispensable goods (Klosko 1992: Ch. 4), or try to find a different basis for other state functions (Klosko 2005: Ch. 5; Wolff 1995: 96–7) (see p. 99).

Second, one might doubt that there is such a thing as an "indispensable" good *simpliciter* (Simmons 1993: 258–9; Wolff 1995: 94–5). It may be true that everyone – or at least everyone who is to be taken seriously – wants peace, security, and law and order, but everything depends on the costs and the manner in which they are provided. Think of pacifists who reject violence and coercion as a means to achieve peace, or anarchists who think that one can have peace without the state. Anarchists may want to privately provide protection services in order to achieve peace, security, and law and order. To require them to contribute could be regarded as a violation of their rights. Klosko's answer is that there is no feasible alternative way of producing indispensable non-excludable goods like national defense or law and order (2005: 61–70), because there is no viable stateless society (see Chapter 7). He concedes, though, that conscientious objection could in rare cases free people from political obligations (2005: 70–4). Pacifists may not have to serve in the military, for example. But he doubts that there will be more than a very few people who have conscientious objections against state production of national defense or law and order and are thus released from political obligations like the obligation to pay taxes.

A third problem is the *particularity objection* that we encountered in Chapter 5. At first sight, this might be surprising, since the fairness principle quite clearly specifies to whom fairness obligations are owed, namely to the other cooperators. But the fairness principle cannot explain why there should be specific bonds among compatriots, since cooperative schemes include non-citizens who live in the state's territory as well (Mason 1997: 433–4). Conversely, some citizens who live abroad are not part of the cooperative scheme of "their" state. A defender of a fairness-based account may concede this and try to combine the fairness-based account with a consent- or community-based account: Fairness is to explain obligations among cooperators, while consent or community is to explain obligations among compatriots (see pp. 73, 100).

Fourth, some insist that the voluntary acceptance criterion is simply essential for a plausible fairness principle (Horton 1992: 95; Simmons 2001: 33–6; Carr 2002: 12; Rinderle 2005: 193–5). If you do not voluntarily accept a good, how can you be said to free ride on other people's efforts? Klosko's answer, of course, is that in the case of indispensable goods we can assume that everyone indeed wants and needs the good. But it is questionable whether this really answers the worry. A *fairness* concern only comes up when people try to free ride on the efforts of others, and it is hard to see how one could unconsciously try to do this.

A possible reply is that a person can still be called a free rider when she *falsely believes* that the non-excludable goods in question could be provided without the state and, for that reason, feels entitled to evade taxes, for example. She may not voluntarily accept the benefits and thus she may indeed not consciously *try* to free ride on other people's efforts, but she is still a free rider, as a matter of fact. There may be some truth in this. When people are culpably unaware of certain relevant facts or hold grossly unreasonable beliefs, then their non-acceptance of non-excludable goods may not free them from fairness obligations, at least under certain conditions (see also Klosko 2014). So voluntary acceptance may indeed not be a *necessary* condition for fairness obligations.

Nevertheless, there are sincere anarchists who do not hold grossly unreasonable beliefs and are not culpably unaware of relevant facts, and yet who do not accept state benefits (see Chapter 7). How could they be regarded as unfair free riders? Second, many people are simply unaware of the relevant state benefits without really being culpable for that; they are not insincere about anything, and they do not hold grossly unreasonable beliefs. It is doubtful whether they are adequately described as free riders in a sense that could explain fairness obligations. For that reason, voluntary acceptance should be regarded as necessary for fairness obligations at least when people are not grossly unreasonable or culpably unaware of relevant facts. A fairness principle that postulates fairness obligations without regard to people's intention to free ride fails to meet the *explanation condition* (even before we take the second step from political obligations to political authority).

From fairness obligations to political authority

But let us assume that Klosko's argument succeeds so far, for the sake of the argument, and that hence all (or almost all) members of a political community have fairness obligations to contribute to the production of indispensable goods like national defense and law and order. How could we get from here to the state's right to rule, its political authority?

But before starting to answer this question, a few words on the *target condition*: The fairness account can certainly not help to explain theoretical authority, since theoretical authority has nothing much to do with cooperation at all. To my knowledge, the fairness account has also not been used to account for obligations or authority relations in families, firms, schools, or religious communities, even though families, firms, schools, and religious communities are certainly joint enterprises in a sense. But if Klosko is right about the relevance of indispensable goods for fairness obligations, then it becomes clear why the fairness principle is most relevant for *political* authority.

Back to the question of how we can get from fairness obligations to state authority: So far we have not assumed that fairness obligations are enforceable. If the state is to have the authority to enact and enforce laws, it must be understood as enforcing people's political obligations. But think of the radio entertainment example again. Arguably, the neighbors may not force me to do a show for them if I refuse, even if I have a fairness obligation to do a show for them. Here the fairness obligation does not seem to be enforceable. Klosko argues that this is different when indispensable goods are at stake, since significant harm is done when indispensable goods are not produced (1992: 45–8). So let us accept that the state may enforce these political obligations.

The next problem for taking the step from political obligations to political authority is that so far all fairness obligations are owed to one's cooperators, the other citizens. Some think that a fairness principle cannot explain political authority, for that reason (Beran 1987: 81–2). It can explain horizontal relations (between citizens), but not vertical relations (between citizens and state).

Yet there is a solution on the horizon. Of course the state and its officials have a role to play in the cooperative scheme that grounds people's political obligations. Could that fact give them moral powers to impose duties on the participants in the scheme? William Edmundson argues that it cannot (2010: 188–90). From the perspective of the fairness principle, the state and its officials must be regarded as useful coordinators in a cooperative scheme. Yet a coordinator does not have a proper power to impose duties, merely a side-effect power to affect people's reasons for action by causally affecting the world (see pp. 10–11). When the state passes a law to drive at 55mph on a particular street, then people do not necessarily have a duty to drive at 55mph on that street, from the perspective of the fairness principle. When people in fact coordinate on driving at 65mph, then the fair-play obligation is to drive at 65mph, not 55mph. This is so, "even if there would have been no drive-65 convention had the state not decreed a lower, 55-mph limit" (Edmundson 2010: 189; see also Himma 2007: 141). In that picture, even though the state affects what citizens have a fairness obligation to do, it does not create content-independent reasons for action for them; there is nothing they have to do just because the state said so. The state lacks a proper power to impose duties. Is that correct?

In reply, Justin Tosi points out that Edmundson neglects how *rules* can specify the terms of cooperation. The rules of the cooperative scheme can empower officials "not merely to propose rules that may then become valid through being practiced. Rather, the rule-given power of their position enables officials to actually create new rules simply by declaring them valid" (2017: 94–5). That rules in cooperative schemes can create authority relations had already been suggested by Hart (in this extended quotation):

> [W]hen a number of persons conduct any joint enterprise according to rules and thus restrict their liberty, those who have submitted to these restrictions when required have a right to a similar submission from those who have benefited by their submission. The rules may provide that officials should have authority to enforce obedience and make further rules, and this will create a structure of legal rights and duties, but the moral obligation to obey the rules in such circumstances is *due to* the co-operating members of the society, and they have the correlative moral right to obedience. (1955: 185; see also Flathman 1980)

Even though political obligations are owed to other members of the cooperative scheme, the scheme may contain rules that assign authority to institutional roles.

Tosi compares the rules of a scheme of cooperation to a contract. Just like a contract specifies how the parties' claim-rights, liberty-rights, etc. are altered via the parties' consent, the rules of a cooperative scheme specify how participation in the cooperative scheme alters the parties' claim-rights, liberty-rights, etc. via the fairness principle. The rules of a cooperative scheme specify new obligations for the parties, but they can also allocate new powers to some roles in the cooperative scheme, including powers to impose duties. Because they are specifying the rules of the scheme of cooperation, all these rights and obligations are morally *validated*. Thus the fairness principle can indeed explain how moral powers to impose duties can come into existence.

This is certainly sophisticated, and yet one may wonder whether rules can really bear the argumentative weight Tosi wants them to bear. I guess the problem is that people's obligations to do their part in a cooperative venture cannot "validate" everything the rules might imply. This would make it rather easy for all kinds of moral powers and claim-rights to simply pop up because people have fairness obligations to do their part in a cooperative enterprise. If the state claims to have a claim-right to be obeyed, would it also be validated? What about the state's power to enact laws in realms that have nothing to do with indispensable goods like national defense? Maybe the answer is that people's fairness obligations validate everything that is essential for providing the relevant indispensable goods.

Another point: Due to the *particularity objection* (p. 91), it is not clear whether the fairness-based argument could fully account for the holistic nature of political authority. The main difficulty is to show that the state has powers not only over cooperators, but also over non-cooperators, including citizens who live abroad. Again, much depends on how the idea of validation is supposed to work. If the cooperative scheme assigns the relevant powers, maybe that is enough to show that the state has them. On the other hand, these powers are certainly not essential for providing indispensable goods.

In any case, recall that the second step in the fairness-based argument for political authority could only succeed because we accepted the success of the first step, for the sake of the argument. We accepted, in other words, that everyone has political obligations based on fairness. But, as we saw earlier, this is doubtful.

Summary

One necessary condition for incurring fairness obligations is that one voluntarily accepts the benefits that are provided through a cooperative enterprise. Because some people do not voluntarily accept the benefits of the state, they cannot be said to have fairness-based political obligations. Some have argued, though, that people can incur fairness obligations *without* voluntarily accepting the benefits, when indispensable goods like law and order are at stake. The worry about this idea is that real fairness concerns only seem to come up when people try to free ride on other people's efforts, and this usually requires voluntary acceptance of the benefits. In any case, even if fairness could explain political obligations, it would still have to explain how these obligations could give rise to a power to impose duties on the side of the state; the rules of the cooperative scheme might be able to help with that task.

7
States without Authority

I have discussed five (families of) theories that attempt to justify political authority. It has been shown that they all face serious objections. Other forms of authority are less problematic: A community-based account seems plausible for the authority of parents, consent theory can explain the authority of bosses, and the service conception may be able to account for theoretical authorities. There have certainly been no last words, and so of course you may think that one of the five theories is on the right track when it comes to political authority as well. In my view, though, the prospects of success are not very good. That is why I would like to examine, in this final chapter, what conclusions we should draw if all five attempts to justify political authority fail.

Alternative theories

Of course I have not been able to discuss *all* attempts to justify political authority. I have focused on what I regard as the most prominent and promising theories. But there are others, and I would like to at least briefly mention them and explain why I think they are not very promising.

One option which I did not discuss is consequentialist theories (Hume 1738: Chs. 3.2.7–10; Flathman 1972: Chs.

7–8; Sartorius 1975: Chs. 5–6; Hare 1976; Goodin 1985: Ch. 5). Although most consequentialist theories focus on political obligation, some have also been applied to political authority. Very roughly, such accounts say that states have political authority if and because their having political authority has good consequences. There are several problems with this idea. One is that consequentialist approaches have trouble in explaining how and why there are particularized moral bonds between states and their citizens (Simmons 1979: 45–54; Horton 1992: Ch. 3; Mason 1997: 434–6). Another problem is that being generally beneficial is arguably irrelevant with regard to individual persons for whom the net result of submission to authority is not beneficial: Even if good consequences could show that the state has authority over some, these consequences could not show that it has authority over those who do not get a net benefit (see Wellman 1996: 213). A final objection is that *if* authority could simply be based on its having desirable consequences, one could establish the same kind of authority for non-state agents like private companies or charity organizations or even individual persons (Huemer 2013: 98–100; Wendt 2016a: 112–16).

A second approach that I have left out is based on the idea of gratitude (Walker 1988; 1989) or respect (Soper 2002). Like consent theory and the fairness principle, the gratitude account has its roots in Plato's *Crito*. It is usually applied to political obligations, not to political authority. The basic thought is that we can understand political obligations as duties of gratitude that we owe to beneficial states. Even if we neglect problems with gratitude as an explanation of political obligations (see Simmons 1979: Ch. 7; Klosko 1989), it seems quite clear that gratitude cannot help to explain political authority. As John Locke pointed out many years ago, owing gratitude to a benefactor does not imply that the benefactor thereby gets the power to impose duties and enact laws for the person she benefited (1689: §70).

Third, one could combine several of the theories presented in Chapters 2–6 and develop a *pluralist* theory (Gans 1992; Wolff 2000; Klosko 2005: Ch. 5). There are two types of pluralism. When applied to political obligations, the first allows that different citizens have their political obligations based on different reasons, while the second claims that all citizens have their political obligations based on the same bundle of reasons. Similarly, when applied to political authority, the first type argues that political authority over some citizens is based on different principles than political authority over others, while the second argues that political authority over all citizens is based on the same set of principles. To do justice to such accounts, one would have to take a closer look at how exactly the different theories from Chapters 2–6 could be combined. Nevertheless, a few remarks may be in place.

I start with the first type of pluralism, the one where the state's authority over some people is based on different grounds than its authority over other people. Certainly such a pluralist theory has a good chance of casting a wider net than theories that have a problem with the *success condition*, like consent theory, the service conception, community-based theories, and fairness-based theories in their voluntarist variant. But remember that most accounts – namely the service conception, community-based theories, natural duty-based theories, and fairness-based theories in their non-voluntarist variant – also have problems with the *explanation condition*, and combining them does not help to overcome *those* problems. The only way to combine theories that do not have serious problems with the *explanation condition* is to rely on consent theory and a fairness-based theory in its voluntarist variant. But while the net will then be wider than the net each theory could cast on its own, the worry is that the net will probably still not be wide enough to catch *everyone*. Yet catching everyone will be necessary if we are to account for the holistic nature of political authority (see p. 7).

What about the second type of pluralism, the one where the state's authority is based on the same grounds in relation to every citizen, but where these grounds refer to several of the theories from Chapters 2–6? One version of this kind of pluralism lets fairness explain the state's authority to enact and enforce laws that help to produce non-excludable goods like peace, security, and law and order, and then lets natural duties of justice explain the state's authority to enact and enforce laws that help to promote justice (see p. 90). But nothing in this way of combining two theories helps to overcome the theories' problems with the *success condition* and the *explanation condition*. On the contrary, combining them in this way presupposes the theories' success and explanatory power in a certain realm.

Another version of this kind of pluralism relies on natural duties or fairness to explain political authority over a particular territory, but uses community considerations (or consent theory) to explain special ties of citizenship (see pp. 73, 91). This may work, as far as it goes, but again it seems that nothing in this way of combining two theories could help to overcome the theories' problems with the *success condition* and the *explanation condition*.

Weak legitimacy

So we should indeed be prepared to accept that all states and very probably all future states lack political authority. A first possible reaction is to argue that political authority is overrated anyway. If we cannot show that states have political authority, then maybe we should simply turn our minds to something weaker that is easier to justify and still sufficient to reconcile us to the state. Therefore, some political philosophers and theorists have advanced weaker notions of political legitimacy, where political legitimacy is not to imply political authority (Smith 1973: 976; Ladenson 1980; Sartorius 1981; Wellman 1996; Edmundson 1998; Morris 1998: Ch. 4; 2005; Buchanan 2002; Zhu 2017). To have political authority means to have the moral power to impose duties. (An even stronger notion of political authority would be to also include a moral claim-right to be obeyed, which I set aside.) Weak political legitimacy, in contrast, is understood as *not* comprising a moral power to impose duties.

There are two basic ways to construe a weaker conception of political legitimacy. One is to replace the power to impose duties with a claim-right against interference with the state's exercise of political power. Another is to go with liberty-rights only, and to simply claim that legitimate states have the liberty-right to enact and enforce (certain kinds of) laws.

Which way is more attractive? William Edmundson points out how odd it would be to conceive the state as having a liberty-right to enforce its laws "while its citizens have not only no duty to obey the law but also no duty not to interfere with the administrative prerogatives by which the law is executed" (1998: 62). Likewise, it would be odd to say that people have the liberty-right to defend themselves, but that others have no duty not to interfere with people's self-defense. This is certainly true; on the other hand, if it is hard to show that states have a power to impose duties on citizens, it may be equally hard to show that states have a claim-right to non-interference with their enforcement of law.

Both weaker notions of political legitimacy are describing a specific status of states, one that is weaker than the status of having legitimate political authority. Sometimes the notion of political legitimacy is used in a completely different sense, basically as the justifiability of particular exercises of political power (Nagel 1987; Rawls 1993: 137, 217, 224; Williams 2005; see also Stark 2000: 323–30). The justifiable exercise of political power need not be based on the permanent status of either being (weakly) legitimate or having political authority. Conversely, one can imagine states that are (weakly) legitimate or have political authority, but try to exercise their political power in an unjustifiable way. So political legitimacy in this sense does not signify a particular normative status that the state and its institutions ought to have. I put this kind of legitimacy to the side and get back to political legitimacy as a normatively weaker status of states.

I have one objection against weak conceptions of legitimacy (for other objections see Raz 1986: 23–30; Klosko 2005: 51–7): If states are to have the moral right to do what they are doing, then they need the moral power to impose duties. They need the moral power to impose duties on citizens because this is what states do when they enact and enforce laws: They impose duties on citizens. If, for example, the parliament passes a law that forbids riding a motorbike without a helmet, then all citizens thereby incur a duty to wear helmets when riding a motorbike. A legitimate state arguably has the moral right to do what states do, and so it needs to have the moral right to impose duties. In other words, it needs political authority in the full sense used throughout this book.

There are two replies to this objection. The first concedes that states – or, more precisely, the people that fill certain roles in state institutions, like members of parliament – may indeed *claim* to impose duties on people. It is part of their self-understanding. But this does *not* imply that legitimate states are to actually have this power, according to Edmundson. He rejects what he calls the "warranty thesis": "If being an X entails claiming to φ, then being a *legitimate* X entails *truly* claiming to φ" (1998: 39). Theoretical authorities may also make claims that are not true without therefore becoming illegitimate. Aristotle was not right about physics, after all (1998: 44–7). Analogously, states that claim to have the power to impose duties may be legitimate even though they do not actually have this power.

I do not find that convincing. A state without the power to impose duties does not simply make a false claim, it just does not have the *right* to do what it does. There is no analogy with theoretical authorities here. If one wants to draw an analogy, then one should think about a theoretical authority that just does not have superior knowledge or expertise; certainly this would undermine its claim to being a legitimate theoretical authority.

The other reply is that the state does not claim to impose *moral* duties, but only *legal* duties, and so a legitimate state does not need a moral power to impose duties, but at best a legal power to impose duties. States may demand obedience, but they need not imply that people have *moral* duties to obey (Zhu 2017).

In response, one can of course deny that states merely claim to impose legal duties, and not moral duties as well (see Raz 1979: 153–9; but see also Kramer 1999: Ch. 4). But let us grant, for the sake of the argument, that states merely claim to impose legal duties. This, it seems to me, would not imply that legitimate states need no moral power to impose duties. It would merely imply that legitimate states need no moral power to impose *moral* duties. They would still need a moral power to impose *legal* duties. If states impose legal duties, and if legitimate states have the moral right to do what they do, then a legitimate state needs the moral right to impose legal duties on people, and this moral right seems to be a moral power. (Some will prefer to describe it as a moral liberty to exercise the legal power to impose legal duties; yet this description would arguably not change the substance of the justificatory task.) Therefore, we should not speak of legitimate states when they do not have political authority including, most importantly, the moral power to impose duties.

A different way to weaken the notion of state legitimacy would be to keep the power to impose duties, but to drop holism (p. 7). All the theories of political authority from Chapters 2–6 had problems in explaining holism. If we were ready to accept that states could have authority over only *some* citizens and *some* people in their territory, all these theories would have an easier job. And indeed, maybe it would be conceivable to deviate from holism by arguing that states do not need the power to impose duties on citizens who are not in their home state's territory (see p. 73). This would mean changing our conception of states and citizenship, but not in a way that would undermine our understanding of what states essentially are. On the other hand, this way of deviating from holism would not rescue any of the theories we have discussed. To further deviate from holism by arguing that states do not even need the power to impose duties on everyone in their territory would be far more radical. States would no longer have territorial authority, only individualized authority relations with some individuals in their territory, but not with others. It is hard to see how such states could still enact "laws" in any proper sense. To have the right to do what states do, states need holistic authority at least over their territory (if not over all citizens).

Philosophical anarchism

If states lack political authority, and if weaker notions of legitimacy will not help, then the next plausible reaction might be to embrace philosophical anarchism (Wolff 1970; Smith 1973; Raz 1979: Ch. 12; Simmons 1979: Ch. 8; 1993: Ch. 8.4; 1996b; 1999; Green 1988). Philosophical anarchists acknowledge that states lack political authority, and they do not introduce a weaker notion of legitimacy, but they do not think that this is reason enough to aim at abolishing the state. This makes them "philosophical" (in contrast to "political") anarchists. Philosophical anarchists embrace the radical philosophical claim that all states are illegitimate without drawing radical political conclusions. For that reason, some regard philosophical anarchism as a "toothless anarchism" (Gans 1992: 90).

Robert Paul Wolff is famous for arguing for philosophical anarchism on a priori grounds (1970). Roughly, he thinks that there is a deep tension between authority and autonomy that makes it impossible for any state to have legitimate authority. This argument has not convinced many people (see Frankfurt 1973; Gans 1992: Ch. 1; Horton 1992: 123–9; Dagger 1997: 62–8). First of all, in the end Wolff himself seems to admit that a consensual state would have legitimate authority (1970: 68–70), which obviously contradicts the main point of a priori anarchism. Second, it is quite implausible that autonomy requires never submitting to authority; after all, we submit to authority every time we go to see the doctor or take advice from an expert.

A much more plausible reason to embrace philosophical anarchism is that all attempts to explain political authority fail (like those in Chapters 2–6). They do not necessarily fail in a way that makes it *impossible* for states to have political authority. Consensual states may indeed have political authority, for example; the problem simply is that there are no states that actually have the consent of the governed, and that there is no reason to be optimistic that there will be any such states in the future. Hence philosophical anarchism.

But does it really make sense to uphold that all states are illegitimate without drawing radical political conclusions? Let me explain John Simmons's position a bit more. Simmons compares the evaluation of states to our evaluation of businesses or companies. We can think that a business does a great job, and we may be able to list its virtues, and yet this has nothing much to do with the rights that company has over us (namely none, until we sign a contract). In the same way, we can think about the virtues and vices of states without thereby saying anything about the rights they have over us (i.e. their political authority). As Simmons puts it: "I take the legitimacy of a state with respect to me and the other moral qualities of a state to be independent variables, just as I take the right of a business to, say, bill me and the charitableness or efficiency of a business to be independent variables" (1996b: 112; see 1999: 136–7).

Of course not all states are equally good. Some are really horrible, some are decent, and some are in between. So what are the virtues of states? Well, we have talked about them in previous chapters. States can help to provide indispensable non-excludable goods like peace, security, and law and order, and they can institutionalize and enforce people's basic liberal rights and thereby help to establish and promote justice and to prevent serious harm (Simmons 1979: 199; 1993: 267; 1999: 136). If a state does a reasonably good job of these things, then it can be regarded as a *justified state*, which means a morally defensible state (1999: 125).

A first objection to philosophical anarchism is that one cannot separate the issues of the justifiability and the legitimacy or authority of a state in the same way as one can separate them in the case of companies. In the case of companies, of course one can acknowledge their moral qualities and their justifiability without any commitment to ascribing any authority over anyone who is not in a contractual relationship with the company. The case of states is different, though, since "unlike a typical company, states depend for their existence upon nonconsensually coercing all those living within their territorial borders" (Wellman 2005: 27).

Second (and relatedly), I think one can make a case for the claim that states without political authority are also *unjust*, which undermines their justifiability (Wendt 2015: 328–32; see also Senor 1987: 263–4). A state without political authority has the legal power to impose legal duties on citizens, but it lacks the corresponding moral power to impose such duties. It does not have the moral right to do what it does, namely impose legal duties. Compare slavery. The essence of slavery is that some people, the slave-owners, have the legal power to impose legal duties on other people, namely their slaves, even though they do not have the corresponding moral power. Now one may argue that slavery is unjust not because of this lack of a moral power in the slave-owners, but because slave-owners violate basic moral rights of their slaves (like when they are exploited, beaten, or killed). But this is not true. Slavery is unjust even when slave-owners are very benevolent and do not violate these basic moral rights of their slaves. We can even assume that slave-owners never exercise the legal powers they have over their slaves, but just let them do whatever they want to do. Still slavery looks unjust, and the reason must lie in the assignment of legal powers that do not correspond with the relevant moral powers. A lack of political authority is therefore not a minor worry, like some philosophical anarchists seem to think. It makes states deeply unjust, and thus it is hard to see how states could lack political authority but nonetheless be justified.

But let us assume, for the sake of the argument, that some states are justified even though they lack political authority. If they are justified, then they will certainly be said to have the liberty-right to do certain things, like enact and enforce laws, even though they do not have a claim to our obedience or a power to impose duties on us. If that is so, then why not call them legitimate in a weak sense? What is the real difference between philosophical anarchism and a weak legitimacy position?

Indeed, some consequences of the two positions are identical. There is no general obligation to obey the law, since we do not have content-independent reasons to obey the law (i.e. reasons to obey the law simply because it is the law). Whether we may disobey or not simply depends on the content of a law. If the law prohibits murder, then of course we should follow the law, albeit not because it is the law, but because murder is morally forbidden. But we may disobey laws that are wrongly enforced (Simmons 1987: 279; 1993: 268; 1996b: 115, 118). All this follows if the state has no moral power to impose duties (or a claim-right to be obeyed), and so it follows both from philosophical anarchism and from a weak legitimacy position. (By the way, it even follows if the state merely has a moral power to impose legal duties, but not moral duties.) Obviously, philosophical anarchism does not imply that we generally have good reason to try to undermine and abolish states, even when they are mildly unjustified states (Simmons 1979: 193–4; 1993: 262–3, 268; 1999: 137).

If the difference between philosophical anarchism and a weak legitimacy position does not lie in people's reasons for obedience and disobedience, then the difference must lie in the state's rights or status. On a weak account of legitimacy, the state has a liberty-right to enact and enforce laws (within certain limits). Even though he thinks that some states are justified, Simmons never says that these states have any such liberty-right. What he does say is that the state is justified in doing certain things, but only because these are things that every individual would be justified in doing as well, like prohibiting murder (1993: 264–5; 1999: 155–6; see also Nozick 1974: 89, 108–9, 114–15). Interestingly, Simmons thinks that this even holds for unjustified states:

> For states may be justified in acting in certain ways on particular occasions, I think, even if they are neither justified nor legitimate – simply because anyone would be justified in so acting. States may be justified on balance in enforcing certain laws, say, even if they are not justified on balance in existing or are not legitimate with respect to those against whom the laws are enforced. (1999: 156)

It seems, then, as if Simmons could drop the idea that there are "justified states" without great costs, but with the benefit of avoiding the above objections. Instead he could exclusively focus on what states are justified *in doing*; and the idea is that states are justified in doing things that everyone would be justified in doing.

So what is the state justified in doing, according to philosophical anarchism? May the state tax its citizens, for example? A weak legitimacy position can say that states have the liberty-right to enact and enforce tax laws, for example, and it can deny that individual citizens have that liberty-right as well. Simmons, on the other hand, denies that states have any rights that individuals lack. He thus has to deny that states have the liberty-right to tax citizens, since individual citizens may not coercively take money from their co-citizens. Indeed he says that taxation wrongs citizens and that disobedience can be justified in the case of taxation (1987: 279; 1993: 265). Yet he also says that "where a government acts without right, it need not act without moral justification" (1987: 278), and "of course, governments may sometimes be justified in coercive interference (if something of moral importance turns on interference)" (1987: 279). As the context makes clear, this coercive interference can take the form of taxation or even conscription.

The next worry about philosophical anarchism, then, is that this justification of taxation does not fit well with the view that the state is only justified in doing what citizens are justified in doing as well. If states can be justified in taxing or conscripting citizens, it is hard to see why citizens should not be said to be justified in taxing or conscripting other citizens as well, on Simmons's account (Windeknecht 2012: 184–5). It is also hard to see why states should not be said to be justified in taxing or conscripting citizens in other states (Windeknecht 2012: 186–7). Thus philosophical anarchism would become more coherent if it stuck to its guns and rejected the justifiability of taxation and conscription, which would bring it closer to political anarchism (which I will discuss in a bit). If, on the other hand, philosophical anarchism wants to take taxation as justified, it would become more coherent if it admitted that states have a liberty-right to tax citizens, a liberty-right that individual citizens lack. This move would let philosophical anarchism collapse into a weak legitimacy position.

A second and related problem of the philosophical anarchist position is that if states may only do what individuals may do as well, then arguably states may not even enact laws, since this is not something every individual may do. As Ryan Windeknecht puts it, "prohibiting rape and punishing rapists is different from creating and enforcing laws and policies which prohibit rape and punish rapists" (2012: 183). Again, a philosophical anarchist may therefore want to ascribe a liberty-right to enact and enforce laws to the state – a right that individuals lack – thereby collapsing the position into a weak legitimacy position.

Political anarchism

If states lack political authority, and if a weak legitimacy position and philosophical anarchism are not viable, then it seems that one has to become a "real" anarchist, i.e.

a political anarchist in contrast to a mere philosophical anarchist. Political anarchists not only think that all states are illegitimate, they also aim at abolishing the state. Not many people are willing to endorse that position, of course. When they think of anarchy, they think of war and chaos, basically as in Thomas Hobbes's state of nature. But political anarchists do not only think that states are illegitimate and unjust, they also think that a peaceful and just stateless society is possible. So let us briefly consider their vision.

Political anarchism comes in a socialist and a capitalist version. Both reject the state, but they differ in the economic institutions they recommend for the stateless society. Socialist anarchism had its advocates in the nineteenth century (Proudhon 1840; Bakunin 1873; Kropotkin 1892), but I will here concentrate on the capitalist version of anarchism, or "free market anarchism" (Molinari 1849; Friedman 1973; Rothbard 1973; Benson 1990; Barnett 1998; Huemer 2013).

For most goods and services from food to cars, we know how they can be produced without the state, since they are actually produced by private companies in our world. The reason why anarchy seems unfeasible is that we cannot imagine how goods like peace, security, and law and order could be provided without the state. Yet the market anarchist's answer is very simple: These goods can be provided by private companies, just like any other goods and services can be provided by private companies. Note that even in our non-anarchist world security is privatized to a considerable degree. People buy burglar alarm systems, they submit to private arbitration in their religious communities, and companies hire private security guards.

But let me flesh out a little bit more how anarchists imagine a free market in the production of security and law and order could work. Competing private protection companies are supposed to do the job that the police do in our countries. Maybe these companies would offer insurance schemes, such that customers paid in advance for their protection. Anarchists think that competition among protection companies would help to provide incentives for better and cheaper protection services. If market competition is healthy in the production of beer and mobile phones, why should it not be healthy in the production of security? Customers who were unhappy with the service of a protection company could choose a different one, and so every protection company would be keen to provide a good service at a reasonable price. With our state police this is different, of course. You cannot choose a different police agency if you are dissatisfied with state police. There is no competition and no voluntarily choosing one agency over another.

Competing arbitration companies are supposed to do the job that the courts do in our countries. The product they are to offer is fair arbitration. Again, because there is competition among arbitration companies, they would have an incentive to try to provide a good service for a good price. Arbitration companies would of course need some *law* to base their decisions on. Where could the law come from in a stateless society? Well, first of all, private property owners and home owner associations could determine the rules that apply to their property. Second, the protection companies might develop codes of conduct ("laws") for their members, and they could also develop laws that regulate the relations to members of other protection companies. Most importantly, such "inter-group" laws would identify arbitrators for conflicts among members of different protection companies.

> [T]here might be many courts and even many legal systems. Each pair of protection agencies agree in advance on which court they will use in case of conflict. Thus the laws under which a particular case is decided are determined implicitly by advance agreement between the protection agencies whose customers are involved. In principle, there could be a different court and a different set of laws for every pair of protection agencies. (Friedman 1973: 117)

Third, the decisions of the arbitrators themselves could count as precedents and thus form the basis of a common law.

Even though anarchists think that it would be desirable to have a stateless society, they need not advocate a violent revolution, of course. Political anarchists can and should be sensitive to moral side-constraints on how to bring about a better and more just social order, and making a violent revolution arguably violates those moral side-constraints. Moreover, anarchists should take care not to worsen the situation, and violent revolutions are usually hard to control.

States without Authority 111

Thus anarchists should advocate peaceful means and incremental change for the better – which means trying to reduce state involvement wherever this is possible (maybe with a priority on reducing state involvement that privileges the rich and powerful). One cannot expect that an anarchist experiment will be possible in the near future.

It is important to see that a stateless society would not be a society without authorities. Of course there would still be theoretical authorities, but also parents, teachers, bosses, and religious leaders would still exercise authority over others. It is only the authority of the state that would be dissolved; but this means that adults would never be subjected to any practical authority except when they submit *voluntarily* (for example by joining a religious community or a protection company).

I think political anarchism should be taken more seriously than it usually is. But of course there are many objections. I will only mention a few central ones, and I will present anarchist replies without being able to fully discuss and assess them here. Whether a stateless society would be viable is not a philosophical question, and it is a question that is beyond the scope of this book. That being said, here are five objections and anarchist replies.

First of all, and most abstractly, many objectors insist that (partly) non-excludable goods like peace, security, and law and order cannot adequately be produced in a market, since people have an incentive to try to free ride on the efforts of others and consume the good without paying for it (Cowen 1992; Morris 1998: Ch. 3; Klosko 2005: Ch. 2). Therefore, we need the state to get such goods.

There have been studies, though, that show how non-excludable goods – for example dams – can and indeed have been provided without the state (Ostrom 1990; Schmidtz 1991). Yet defenders of the state will contend that peace, security, and law and order are special. One reason why they are special may be that the "nature of the service brings different [private protection] agencies not only into competition for customers' patronage, but also into violent conflict with each other" (Nozick 1974: 17). Robert Nozick argues that the protection company which wins the fights will become more and more attractive, and in the end be the only game in town.

Thus a system of competing protection agencies will eventually evolve into a system where protection companies have local monopolies in their territory and become quite similar to states, according to Nozick (1974: 15–17, 113–18). But why should competing protection companies get into violent conflict with each other in the first place? One reason could be that some of the protection agencies become outlaw firms and simply try to make money by robbing others. But there may also be more structural reasons for the likelihood of violent conflicts among competing protection companies. As Christopher Wellman puts it, since "people would select agencies for self-interested reasons, they would seek agencies that best protect their clients. A problem arises, then, since maximally protecting clients could require a company to disrespect the moral rights of nonclients" (1996: 232; see 2001: 743; 2005: 15–16).

Anarchists will reply that this gets the incentives wrong. For one thing, violent conflict is very costly and nothing any customer would want, so protection companies would try to avoid such conflicts. Second, there is a wide consensus about the basic moral rights of people, and so a protection company that openly disrespected these rights would probably face resistance from many people, and it would lose most customers. For the same reasons, the system of competing private protection companies is not very *likely* to devolve into a gang war. Of course, it is *possible* that very bad things happen in a stateless society. But, on the other hand, it is also possible that states commit murderous crimes against their citizens. In fact, this has happened quite regularly in history, as we all know.

A second worry is that a system of competing law codes would be confusing, incomprehensible, and inefficient (see Miller 2002: 25). The law is to provide a stable framework for people's lives, and this arguably requires a state monopoly in the production of law (see Hayek 1960).

One anarchist answer to this challenge is that there might actually evolve a relatively homogenous code of law in a stateless society, because customers will prefer protection and arbitration companies that offer widely accepted regulations for conflicts between members of different companies. These regulations would most likely institutionalize the most widely accepted moral norms (against killing, stealing, fraud, etc.).

Another answer is to turn the tables on the defender of the state, and point to the overproduction of law in actual states. According to Michael Huemer (2013: 280–1), federal regulation in the United States grew from 22,877 pages in 1960 to 152,456 pages in 2010. From the sheer numbers, it is quite plausible to infer that the rule of law in the United States (and in other contemporary states) is far from efficient, transparent, and comprehensible. The problem is that the overproduction of law comes with economic costs and leads to massively increased costs for the application of the law in courts. In our states, one needs special expertise to understand even one small segment of the law. In a stateless society, in contrast, there is no incentive for an overproduction of law – customers will not appreciate it, after all – and so the system of law in a stateless society might in the end provide a more transparent and comprehensible framework than the framework we have in our current states.

A third worry is that poor people might not be able to afford private protection and private arbitration. The quite simple and self-confident anarchist reply is that (for reasons explained earlier) there will be better and cheaper security services and less poor people in a well-working stateless society. If necessary, private charity will take care that no one is left without protection. Such charity organizations might give out vouchers for poor people that allow them to join protection and arbitration companies of their choice. Alternatively, they could be non-profit organizations that themselves provide protection and arbitration. Many people will be willing to support such charity organizations with their donations. That, at least, is what one should hope.

Fourth, even if police and courts could be privatized, there remains the problem of national defense. How could a stateless society be protected against foreign aggression? An anarchist may point out that one should not underrate the effectiveness of guerilla warfare and the deterrent effect of an armed population. In any case, much will depend on historical circumstances; it matters whether the anarchist society enjoys protection from powerful states, for example.

Fifth, many people will think that history teaches us that anarchism does not work. The anarchist vision of society is a utopian dreamland. Wherever states have collapsed or lost control over some territory, we have seen not prosperity and justice, but chaos, violence, and starvation. Somalia or Syria might be recent cases in point.

Anarchists will reply that pointing to Somalia or Syria is unfair, since a working anarchist society obviously needs appropriate institutions and cultural preconditions. This reply may remind you of communists who argue that "real communism" has never been tried and is not refuted by the terrible reality of real-world communism (or socialism). While anarchists can at least point to some historical examples of relatively well-working stateless societies like medieval Iceland (Friedman 1979), it indeed seems hard to find examples of well-working anarchist societies in the modern world. Without such examples, one has good reason to be cautious about advocating anarchism. On the other hand, the ideal of a democratic state was also denounced as a utopian dreamland for many centuries, and it took a long time until humanity saw examples of well-working modern democracies. Who knows what the future of the ideal of a stateless society will be.

Summary

If all the theories from Chapters 2–6 fail, then one has three main options. First, one can work with a weaker notion of legitimacy that does not include a power to impose duties. The problem is that the state needs that power in order to have the right to do what it does. Second, one can become a philosophical anarchist who thinks that even illegitimate states can be justified in doing certain things. But philosophical anarchism tends to collapse into a weak legitimacy position. Third, one can become a political anarchist and advocate a stateless society. Here, the decisive question is how plausible it is that the institutions of a stateless society would be more just and efficient than our current institutions.

Bibliography

Anderson, Elizabeth 2017: *Private Government: How Employers Rule Our Lives (and Why We Don't Talk about It)*. Princeton: Princeton University Press.
Anscombe, Elizabeth 1978: On the Source of the Authority of the State. *Ratio* 20: 1–28.
Applbaum, Arthur I. 2010: Legitimacy without the Duty to Obey. *Philosophy & Public Affairs* 38: 215–39.
Aristotle 2013: *Politics* (ed. and trans. C. Lord). Chicago: Chicago University Press.
Arneson, Richard J. 1982: The Principle of Fairness and Free-Rider Problems. *Ethics* 92: 616–33.
Badhwar, Neera 1991: Why It Is Wrong to Be Always Guided by the Best: Consequentialism and Friendship. *Ethics* 101: 483–504.
Bakunin, Mikhail 1873/1990: *Statism and Anarchy* (ed. and trans. M. Shatz). Cambridge: Cambridge University Press.
Barnett, Randy E. 1998: *The Structure of Liberty: Justice and the Rule of Law*. Oxford: Oxford University Press.
Bell, Nora K. 1978: Nozick and the Principle of Fairness. *Social Theory and Practice* 5: 65–73.
Benson, Bruce L. 1990/2011: *The Enterprise of Law: Justice without the State*. Oakland: Independent Institute.
Beran, Harry 1977: In Defense of the Consent Theory of Political Obligation and Authority. *Ethics* 87: 260–71.
Beran, Harry 1987: *The Consent Theory of Political Obligation*. London: Croom Helm.
Blake, Michael 2001: Distributive Justice, State Coercion, and Autonomy. *Philosophy & Public Affairs* 30: 257–96.

Buchanan, Allen 2002: Political Legitimacy and Democracy. *Ethics* 112: 689–719.
Carr, Craig 2002: Fairness and Political Obligation. *Social Theory and Practice* 28: 1–28.
Cherry, Mark J. 2010: Parental Authority and Pediatric Bioethical Decision Making. *Journal of Medicine and Philosophy* 35: 553–72.
Christiano, Thomas 2004: The Authority of Democracy. *Journal of Political Philosophy* 12: 266–90.
Christiano, Thomas 2008: *The Constitution of Equality: Democratic Authority and Its Limits*. Oxford: Oxford University Press.
Cohen, Joshua 1989: Deliberation and Democratic Legitimacy. In A. Hamlin and P. Pettit (eds.): *The Good Polity: Normative Analysis of the State*. New York: Blackwell, pp. 17–34.
Copp, David 1999: The Idea of a Legitimate State. *Philosophy & Public Affairs* 28: 3–45.
Cowen, Tyler 1992: Law as a Public Good: The Economics of Anarchy. *Economics and Philosophy* 8: 249–67.
Dagger, Richard 1997: *Civic Virtues: Rights, Citizenship, and Republican Liberalism*. New York: Oxford University Press.
Dagger, Richard 2000: Membership, Fair Play, and Political Obligation. *Political Studies* 48: 104–17.
Darwall, Stephen 2009: Authority and Second-Personal Reasons for Acting. In D. Sobel and S. Wall (eds.): *Reasons for Action*. Cambridge: Cambridge University Press, pp. 134–54.
Darwall, Stephen 2010: Authority and Reasons: Exclusionary and Second-Personal. *Ethics* 120: 257–78.
de Puydt, Paul-Émile 1860/2016. Panarchy (trans. J. Zube and A. Tucker). In A. Tucker and G. de Bellis (eds.): *Panarchy: Political Theories of Non-Territorial States*. London: Routledge, pp. 21–36.
Dietrich, Frank 2014: Consent as the Foundation of Political Authority: A Lockean Perspective. *Rationality, Markets and Morals* 5: 64–78.
Dworkin, Ronald 1973: The Original Position. *University of Chicago Law Review* 40: 500–33.
Dworkin, Ronald 1986: *Law's Empire*. Cambridge, MA: Harvard University Press.
Edmundson, William 1998: *Three Anarchical Fallacies*. Cambridge: Cambridge University Press.
Edmundson, William 2010: Political Authority, Moral Powers and the Intrinsic Value of Obedience. *Oxford Journal of Legal Studies* 30: 179–91.
Edmundson, William 2011: Consent and its Cousins. *Ethics* 121: 335–53.

Enoch, David 2011: Reason-Giving and the Law. In L. Green and B. Leiter (eds.): *Oxford Studies in Philosophy of Law* 1. Oxford: Oxford University Press, pp. 1–38.
Enoch, David 2014: Authority and Reason-Giving. *Philosophy and Phenomenological Research* 96: 296–332.
Essert, Christopher 2015: Legal Powers in Private Law. *Legal Theory* 21: 136–55.
Estlund, David 2008: *Democratic Authority*. Princeton: Princeton University Press.
Filmer, Robert 1680/1991: *Patriarcha and other Writings* (ed. J. Sommerville). Cambridge: Cambridge University Press.
Flathman, Richard 1972: *Political Obligation*. New York: Atheneum.
Flathman, Richard 1980: *The Practice of Authority: Authority and the Authoritative*. Chicago: Chicago University Press.
Frankfurt, Harry 1973: The Anarchism of Robert Paul Wolff. *Political Theory* 1: 405–14.
Friedman, David 1973/1989: *The Machinery of Freedom: Guide to a Radical Capitalism*, 2nd edition. LaSalle: Open Court.
Friedman, David 1979: Private Creation and Enforcement of Law: A Historical Case. *Journal of Legal Studies* 8: 399–415.
Gans, Chaim 1992: *Philosophical Anarchism and Political Disobedience*. Cambridge: Cambridge University Press.
Gaus, Gerald 2011: *The Order of Public Reason: A Theory of Freedom and Morality in a Diverse and Bounded World*. Cambridge: Cambridge University Press.
Gauthier, David 1986: *Morals by Agreement*. Oxford: Oxford University Press.
Gheaus, Anca 2017: Children's Vulnerability and Legitimate Authority over Children. *Journal of Applied Philosophy* (doi: 10.1111/japp.12262).
Gilbert, Margaret 2006: *A Theory of Political Obligation*. Oxford: Oxford University Press.
Gilbert, Margaret 2013: *Joint Commitment: How We Make the Social World*. Oxford: Oxford University Press.
Goodin, Robert E. 1985: *Protecting the Vulnerable: A Reanalysis of our Social Responsibilities*. Chicago: Chicago University Press.
Goodin, Robert E. 1988: What is So Special about Our Fellow Countrymen? *Ethics* 98: 663–86.
Green, Leslie 1988: *The Authority of the State*. Oxford: Oxford University Press.
Greenawalt, Kent 1987: *Conflicts of Law and Morality*. Oxford: Oxford University Press.
Greene, Amanda 2016: Consent and Political Legitimacy. In D. Sobel, P. Vallentyne, and S. Wall (eds.): *Oxford Studies in*

Political Philosophy 2. Oxford: Oxford University Press, pp. 71–97.

Habermas, Jürgen 1992/1996: *Between Facts and Norms: Contributions to a Discourse Theory of Law and Democracy* (trans. W. Rehg). Cambridge, MA: MIT Press.

Haidt, Jonathan 2012: *The Righteous Mind: Why Good People are Divided by Politics and Religion*. London: Penguin.

Hardimon, Michael 1994: Role Obligations. *Journal of Philosophy* 91: 333–63.

Hare, Richard M. 1976: Political Obligation. In T. Honderich (ed.): *Social Ends and Political Means*. London: Routledge & Kegan Paul, pp. 1–12.

Hart, H. L. A. 1955: Are There Any Natural Rights? *Philosophical Review* 64: 175–91.

Hart, H. L. A. 1961/1994: *The Concept of Law*. Oxford: Oxford University Press.

Hayek, Friedrich A. 1960: *The Constitution of Liberty*. Chicago: Chicago University Press.

Hershovitz, Scott 2003: Legitimacy, Democracy, and Razian Authority. *Legal Theory* 9: 201–20.

Himma, Kenneth E. 2007: Just 'Cause You're Smarter than Me Doesn't Give You a Right to Tell Me What to Do: Legitimate Authority and the Normal Justification Thesis. *Oxford Journal of Legal Studies* 27: 121–50.

Hobbes, Thomas 1651/1996: *Leviathan* (ed. J. Gaskin). Oxford: Oxford University Press.

Hohfeld, Wesley N. 1913/2001: *Fundamental Legal Conceptions as Applied in Judicial Reasoning* (eds. D. Campbell and P. Thomas). Burlington: Ashgate.

Horton, John 1992/2010: *Political Obligation*, 2nd edition. Basingstoke: Palgrave Macmillan.

Horton, John 2012: Political Legitimacy, Justice and Consent. *Critical Review of International Social and Political Philosophy* 15: 129–48.

Horton, John and Ryan G. Windeknecht 2015: Is There a Distinctively Associative Account of Political Obligation? *Political Studies* 63: 903–18.

Huemer, Michael 2013: *The Problem of Political Authority: An Examination of the Right to Coerce and the Duty to Obey*. London: Palgrave Macmillan.

Hume, David 1738/1978: *A Treatise of Human Nature* (eds. L. Selby-Bigge and P. Nidditch). Oxford: Clarendon Press.

Hume, David 1748/1994: Of the Original Contract. In *Political Essays* (ed. K. Haakonssen). Cambridge: Cambridge University Press, pp. 186–201.

Hurd, Heidi M. 1991: Challenging Authority. *Yale Law Journal* 100: 1611–83.
Jeske, Diane 2001: Special Relationships and the Problem of Political Obligations. *Social Theory and Practice* 27: 19–40.
Kant, Immanuel 1793/2006: On the Common Saying: That May Be Correct in Theory, but It Is of No Use in Practice. In *Practical Philosophy* (ed. and trans. M. Gregor). Cambridge: Cambridge University Press, pp. 273–310.
Kant, Immanuel 1797/2006. *The Metaphysics of Morals*. In *Practical Philosophy* (ed. and trans. M. Gregor). Cambridge: Cambridge University Press, pp. 353–604.
Kavka, Gregory S. 1986: *Hobbesian Moral and Political Theory*. Princeton: Princeton University Press.
Keller, Simon 2013: *Partiality*. Princeton: Princeton University Press.
Kelsen, Hans 1934/1967: *Pure Theory of Law*, 2nd edition (trans. M. Knight). Berkeley: University of California Press.
Klosko, George 1989: Political Obligation and Gratitude. *Philosophy & Public Affairs* 18: 352–8.
Klosko, George 1992: *The Principle of Fairness and Political Obligation*. Lanham: Rowman & Littlefield.
Klosko, George 2005: *Political Obligations*. Oxford: Oxford University Press.
Klosko, George 2014: Fairness Obligations and Non-Acceptance of Benefits. *Political Studies* 62: 159–71.
Knowles, Dudley 2010: *Political Obligation: A Critical Introduction*. London: Routledge.
Kolodny, Niko 2014: Rule over None. *Philosophy & Public Affairs* 42: 195–229 (Part One) and 287–336 (Part Two).
Koltonski, Daniel 2013: Normative Consent and Authority. *Journal of Moral Philosophy* 10: 255–75.
Kramer, Matthew 1999: *In Defence of Legal Positivism: Law without Trimmings*. Oxford: Oxford University Press.
Kropotkin, Peter 1892/1995: *The Conquest of Bread and Other Writings* (ed. and trans. M. Shatz). Cambridge: Cambridge University Press.
Ladenson, Robert 1980: In Defense of a Hobbesian Conception of Law. *Philosophy & Public Affairs* 9: 134–59.
Lazar, Seth 2016: The Justification of Associative Duties. *Journal of Moral Philosophy* 13: 28–55.
Lefkowitz, David 2005: A Contractualist Defense of Democratic Authority. *Ratio Juris* 18: 346–64.
Locke, John 1689/1960: Second Treatise of Government. In *Two Treatises of Government* (ed. P. Laslett). Cambridge: Cambridge University Press, pp. 265–428.

Macdonald, Margaret 1941: The Language of Political Theory. *Proceedings of the Aristotelian Society* 41: 91–112.
Marmor, Andrei 2005: Authority, Equality and Democracy. *Ratio Juris* 18: 315–45.
Mason, Andrew 1997: Special Obligations to Compatriots. *Ethics* 107: 427–47.
McMahon, Christopher 1994: *Authority and Democracy: A General Theory of Government and Management*. Princeton: Princeton University Press.
McPherson, Thomas 1967: *Political Obligation*. London: Routledge & Kegan Paul.
Milgram, Stanley 1974: *Obedience to Authority: An Experimental View*. New York: Harper.
Miller, David 1995: *On Nationality*. Oxford: Clarendon Press.
Miller, David 2002: The Justification of Political Authority. In D. Schmidtz (ed.): *Robert Nozick*. Cambridge: Cambridge University Press, pp. 10–33.
Mokrosinska, Dorota 2012: *Rethinking Political Obligation: Moral Principles, Communal Ties, Citizenship*. Basingstoke: Palgrave Macmillan.
Molinari, Gustave de 1849/2009: *The Production of Security* (ed. R. Ebeling, trans. J. McCulloch). Auburn: Ludwig von Mises Institute.
Morris, Christopher 1998: *An Essay on the Modern State*. Cambridge: Cambridge University Press.
Morris, Christopher 2005: Natural Rights and Political Legitimacy. *Social Philosophy and Policy* 22: 314–29.
Murphy, Mark 1999: Surrender of Judgment and the Consent Theory of Political Obligation. *Law and Philosophy* 16: 115–43.
Nagel, Thomas 1987: Moral Conflict and Political Legitimacy. *Philosophy & Public Affairs* 16: 215–40.
Nozick, Robert 1974: *Anarchy, State, and Utopia*. New York: Basic Books.
Ostrom, Elinor 1990: *Governing the Commons: The Evolution of Institutions for Collective Action*. Cambridge: Cambridge University Press.
Pateman, Carole 1979: *The Problem of Political Obligation: A Critical Analysis of Liberal Theory*. Los Angeles: University of California Press.
Perry, Stephen 2005: Law and Obligation. *American Journal of Jurisprudence* 50: 263–95.
Peter, Fabienne 2008: *Democratic Legitimacy*. London: Routledge.
Pitkin, Hanna 1965: Obligation and Consent. *American Political Science Review* 59: 990–9 (Part One) and 60: 39–52 (Part Two).

Plamenatz, John 1938/1968: *Consent, Freedom, and Political Obligation*, 2nd edition. Oxford: Oxford University Press.
Plato 1981/2002: Crito. In *Five Dialogues: Euthyphro, Apology, Crito, Meno, Phaedo*, 2nd edition (ed. J. Cooper, trans. G. Grube). Indianapolis: Hackett, pp. 45–57.
Proudhon, Pierre-Joseph 1840/1979: *What Is Property?* (eds. and trans. D. Kelly and B. Smith). Cambridge: Cambridge University Press.
Quong, Jonathan 2011: *Liberalism without Perfection*. Oxford: Oxford University Press.
Railton, Peter 1984: Alienation, Consequentialism, and the Demands of Morality. *Philosophy & Public Affairs* 13: 134–71.
Rawls, John 1964/1999: Legal Obligation and the Principle of Fair Play. In *Collected Papers* (ed. S. Freeman). Harvard: Harvard University Press, pp. 117–29.
Rawls, John 1971: *A Theory of Justice*. Cambridge, MA: Harvard University Press.
Rawls, John 1993: *Political Liberalism*. New York: Columbia University Press.
Raz, Joseph 1975/1999: *Practical Reason and Norms*. Oxford: Oxford University Press.
Raz, Joseph 1979: *The Authority of Law*. Oxford: Oxford University Press.
Raz, Joseph 1984/1994: The Obligation to Obey: Revision and Tradition. In *Ethics in the Public Domain*. Oxford: Clarendon Press, pp. 341–54.
Raz, Joseph 1985/1994: Authority, Law, and Morality. In *Ethics in the Public Domain*. Oxford: Clarendon Press, pp. 210–37.
Raz, Joseph 1986: *The Morality of Freedom*. Oxford: Clarendon Press.
Raz, Joseph 2006: The Problem of Authority: Revisiting the Service Conception. *Minnesota Law Review* 90: 1003–44.
Raz, Joseph 2010: On Respect, Authority, and Neutrality: A Response. *Ethics* 120: 279–301.
Renzo, Massimo 2008: Duties of Samaritanism and Political Obligation. *Legal Theory* 14: 193–217.
Renzo, Massimo 2012: Associative Responsibilities and Political Obligations. *Philosophical Quarterly* 62: 106–27.
Renzo, Massimo 2014: Fairness, Self-Deception and Political Obligation. *Philosophical Studies* 169: 467–88.
Rinderle, Peter 2005: *Der Zweifel des Anarchisten: Für eine neue Theorie vom politischer Verpflichtung und staatlicher Legitimität*. Frankfurt: Vittorio Klostermann.
Rothbard, Murray 1973/1978: *For a New Liberty: The Libertarian Manifesto*, 2nd edition. New York: Collier.

Rousseau, Jean-Jacques 1762/1968: *The Social Contract* (ed. and trans. M. Cranston). London: Penguin.
Sartorius, Rolf 1975: *Individual Conduct and Social Norms*. Belmont: Dickenson.
Sartorius, Rolf 1981: Political Authority and Political Obligation. *Virginia Law Review* 67: 3–17.
Scanlon, Thomas 1998: *What We Owe to Each Other*. Cambridge, MA: Harvard University Press.
Scheffler, Samuel 1997/2002: Relationships and Responsibilities. In *Boundaries and Allegiances: Problems of Justice and Responsibility in Liberal Thought*. Oxford: Oxford University Press, pp. 97–110.
Schmelzle, Cord 2015: *Politische Legitimität und zerfallene Staatlichkeit*. Frankfurt: Campus.
Schmidtz, David 1991: *The Limits of Government: An Essay on the Public Goods Argument*. Boulder: Westview Press.
Seglow, Jonathan 2013: *Defending Associative Duties*. London: Routledge.
Senor, Thomas 1987: What If There Are No Political Obligations? A Reply to A. J. Simmons. *Philosophy & Public Affairs* 16: 260–8.
Sherman, James 2010: Unresolved Problems in the Service Conception of Authority. *Oxford Journal of Legal Studies* 30: 419–40.
Simmons, A. John 1979: *Moral Principles and Political Obligations*. Princeton: Princeton University Press.
Simmons, A. John 1987: The Anarchist Position: A Reply to Klosko and Senor. *Philosophy & Public Affairs* 16: 269–79.
Simmons, A. John 1993: *On the Edge of Anarchy*. Princeton: Princeton University Press.
Simmons, A. John 1996a/2001: Associative Obligations. In *Justification and Legitimacy*. Cambridge: Cambridge University Press, pp. 65–92.
Simmons, A. John 1996b/2001: Philosophical Anarchism. In *Justification and Legitimacy*. Cambridge: Cambridge University Press, pp. 102–21.
Simmons, A. John 1998/2001: "Denisons" and "Aliens": Locke's Problem of Political Consent. In *Justification and Legitimacy*. Cambridge: Cambridge University Press, pp. 158–78.
Simmons, A. John 1999/2001: Justification and Legitimacy. In *Justification and Legitimacy*. Cambridge: Cambridge University Press, pp. 122–57.
Simmons, A. John 2001: Fair Play and Political Obligation: Twenty Years Later. In *Justification and Legitimacy*. Cambridge: Cambridge University Press, pp. 27–42.

Simmons, A. John 2005: The Duty to Obey and our Natural Moral Duties. In C. Wellman and A. J. Simmons: *Is There a Duty to Obey the Law?* Cambridge: Cambridge University Press, pp. 93–196.
Singer, Peter 1974: *Democracy and Disobedience*. Oxford: Oxford University Press.
Smith, M. B. E. 1973: Is There a Prima Facie Obligation to Obey the Law? *Yale Law Journal* 82: 950–76.
Soper, Philip 2002: *The Ethics of Deference: Learning from Law's Morals*. Cambridge: Cambridge University Press.
Sreenivasan, Gopal 2009: "Oh, but You Should Have": Estlund on Normative Consent. *Iyyun* 58: 62–72.
Stark, Cynthia 2000: Hypothetical Consent and Justification. *Journal of Philosophy* 97: 313–34.
Steinberger, Peter 2004: *The Idea of the State*. Cambridge: Cambridge University Press.
Stilz, Anna 2009: *Liberal Loyalty: Freedom, Obligation, and the State*. Princeton: Princeton University Press.
Tamir, Yael 1993: *Liberal Nationalism*. Princeton: Princeton University Press.
Tosi, Justin 2017: The Possibility of a Fair Play Account of Legitimacy. *Ratio* 30: 88–99.
Tussman, Joseph 1960: *Obligation and the Body Politic*. Oxford: Oxford University Press.
van der Vossen, Bas 2011: Associative Obligations: Their Potential. *Philosophy Compass* 6: 488–96.
Vernon, Richard 2007: Obligation by Association? A Reply to John Horton. *Political Studies* 55: 865–79.
Viehoff, Daniel 2011: Procedure and Outcome in the Justification of Authority. *Journal of Political Philosophy* 19: 248–59.
Viehoff, Daniel 2014: Democratic Equality and Political Authority. *Philosophy & Public Affairs* 42: 337–75.
Waldron, Jeremy 1987: Theoretical Foundations of Liberalism. *Philosophical Quarterly* 37: 127–50.
Waldron, Jeremy 1993: Special Ties and Natural Duties. *Philosophy & Public Affairs* 22: 3–30.
Waldron, Jeremy 1999: *Law and Disagreement*. Oxford: Oxford University Press.
Walker, A. D. M. 1988: Political Obligation and the Argument from Gratitude. *Philosophy & Public Affairs* 17: 191–211.
Walker, A. D. M. 1989: Obligations of Gratitude and Political Obligation. *Philosophy & Public Affairs* 18: 359–64.
Wall, Steven 2006: Democracy, Authority and Publicity. *Journal of Political Philosophy* 14: 85–100.

Walzer, Michael 1970: Political Alienation and Military Service. In *Political Obligation: Essays on Disobedience, War, and Citizenship*. Cambridge, MA: Harvard University Press, pp. 99–119.

Weale, Albert 2017: Associative Obligation and the Social Contract. *Philosophia* 45: 463–76.

Weber, Max 1921/1978: *Economy and Society* (eds. and trans. G. Roth and C. Wittich). Berkeley: University of California Press.

Wellman, Christopher H. 1996: Liberalism, Samaritanism, and Political Legitimacy. *Philosophy & Public Affairs* 25: 211–37.

Wellman, Christopher H. 1997: Associative Allegiances and Political Obligations. *Social Theory and Practice* 23: 181–204.

Wellman, Christopher H. 2000: Relational Facts in Liberal Political Theory: Is There Magic in the Pronoun "My"? *Ethics* 110: 537–62.

Wellman, Christopher H. 2001: Toward a Liberal Theory of Political Obligation. *Ethics* 111: 735–59.

Wellman, Christopher H. 2005: Samaritanism and the Duty to Obey the Law. In C. Wellman and A. J. Simmons: *Is There a Duty to Obey the Law?* Cambridge: Cambridge University Press, pp. 1–89.

Wendt, Fabian 2015: Justice and Political Authority in Left-Libertarianism. *Politics, Philosophy & Economics* 14: 316–39.

Wendt, Fabian 2016a: Political Authority and the Minimal State. *Social Theory and Practice* 42: 97–122.

Wendt, Fabian 2016b: On Realist Legitimacy. *Social Philosophy and Policy* 32: 227–45.

Williams, Bernard 2005: *In the Beginning Was the Deed*. Princeton: Princeton University Press.

Windeknecht, Ryan G. 2012: Law without Legitimacy or Justification? The Flawed Foundations of Philosophical Anarchism. *Res Publica* 18: 173–88.

Wolff, Jonathan 1995: Political Obligation, Fairness and Independence. *Ratio* 8: 87–99.

Wolff, Jonathan 2000: Political Obligation: A Pluralistic Approach. In M. Baghramian and A. Ingram (eds.): *Pluralism: The Philosophy and Politics of Diversity*. London: Routledge, pp. 179–96.

Wolff, Robert P. 1970: *In Defense of Anarchism*. New York: Harper & Row.

Zagzebski, Linda T. 2012: *Epistemic Authority: A Theory of Trust, Authority, and Autonomy in Belief*. Oxford: Oxford University Press.

Zhu, Jiafeng 2017: Farewell to Political Obligation: In Defense of a Permissive Conception of Legitimacy. *Pacific Philosophical Quarterly* 98: 449–69.

Index

anarchism
  as a challenge for theories of political authority, 29, 65, 72, 80–1, 90, 92
  defined, 103–4, 109
  and national defense, 113
  and non-excludable goods, 111
  and peace, security, and law and order, 109–14
  philosophical, 103–9
  political, 108–14
  weak legitimacy and philosophical, 106–8
Anderson, Elizabeth, 18
Anscombe, Elizabeth, 74
Applbaum, Arthur I., 9
Aristotle, 61, 102
Arneson, Richard J., 89
authority
  and autonomy, 1, 44, 62, 104
  -based reasons, 2, 3, 5, 10–11, 40–4, 75, 94, 106
  of bosses, 4, 14, 18, 32, 39, 57, 69, 92, 97, 111
  community-based theory of, 50–65, 68, 70–1, 73, 91, 97, 99–100
  consent theory of, 17–36, 39, 45, 48, 57–8, 60, 64–5, 70–1, 79, 83, 86, 91, 94, 97–100, 104
  de facto, 4–6, 38, 43, 62–3
  defined, 3–4
  and equality, 13–14, 18–21, 36, 63, 76–8
  of law, 43
  legitimate vs. de facto, 4–6, 11–12, 62–3
  moral limits to, 11, 18–20, 32, 43, 53, 62, 75, 95, 107
  of parents, 2–4, 14, 19–20, 38–9, 45, 53–5, 57–9, 61–3, 69, 92, 97, 111
  practical vs. theoretical, 1–6, 40–5
  of religious leaders, 4, 14, 18, 57–8, 69, 92, 111
  service conception of, 37–49, 54, 97, 99
  and superior standing, 3–5, 13, 102

authority (*cont.*)
  of teachers, 4, 14, 18–19, 39, 45, 58, 69, 92, 111
  theoretical, 1–5, 18–19, 38, 42–7, 57, 69, 92, 97, 102, 111

Badhwar, Neera, 52
Bakunin, Mikhail, 109
Barnett, Randy E., 109
Bell, Nora K., 85
Benson, Bruce L., 109
Beran, Harry, 26–8, 34, 90, 93
Blake, Michael, 52
Buchanan, Allen, 19–20, 68, 70, 73, 78, 100

Carr, Craig, 90–1
Cherry, Mark, 53
Christiano, Thomas, 7, 20, 46, 72, 76–8
Churchill, Winston, 76
Cohen, Joshua, 78
community
  -based theory of (political) authority, 50–65, 68, 70–1, 73, 91, 97, 99–100
  and consent theory, 63–5
  and consequentialism, 52–3
  and cosmopolitanism, 62, 65
  defined, 50–5
  familial, 50–63, 92
  and identification, 55–7, 60, 64
  and justice, 58–60
  moral bonds in, 50–63, 70–3, 78, 81, 91, 98, 100
  and partiality, 52–3
  political, 12, 26, 50, 52, 54–65, 70–3, 80, 91–2
  and political obligation, 54–5, 59, 65
  and the power to impose duties, 55, 63–5
  true, 59–60
consent
  and acceptability, 29–31
  vs. acceptance, 64–5
  -based theory of (political) authority, 17–36, 39, 45, 48, 57–8, 60, 64–5, 70–1, 79, 83, 86, 91, 94, 97–100, 104
  coerced, 23–8, 31, 34–5
  defined, 17–18
  and dissenters' territories, 28, 34
  and emigration, 25–8, 34
  explicit, 17–22, 25, 34
  hypothetical, 29–31, 79
  as an ideal, 35–6
  and inheritance, 25–6
  and institutional reform, 26, 28, 34–5
  and non-excludable goods, 34
  normative, 31–3
  and the original contract, 17, 21, 24, 32
  and political obligation, 26, 34, 36
  as a power to create rights, 17–19, 22, 30–1, 33, 64
  and the power to impose duties, 18, 22, 28, 30–2
  tacit, 22–8, 34, 65, 86
  and voting, 25–6, 28, 34
Copp, David, 9, 74
Cowen, Tyler, 111

Dagger, Richard, 58–60, 62, 85, 89, 104
Darwall, Stephan, 46
de Puydt, Paul-Émile, 34
Declaration of Independence, 21
Dietrich, Frank, 34
duty, *see* natural duty
Dworkin, Ronald, 29, 59

Edmundson, William, 10, 32, 93–4, 100–2
Enoch, David, 9–10
Essert, Christopher, 10
Estlund, David, 10, 31–3, 74, 79

fairness
  and acceptance of benefits, 83, 85–9, 91–2
  -based theory of political authority, 80, 83–95, 98–100
  defined, 83–4, 87
  and indispensable goods, 89–93, 95
  and non-excludable goods, 85–7, 89–92, 99
  and the particularity objection, 91, 95
  and political obligation, 80, 87–8, 90–1, 93–5
  and the power to impose duties, 93–5
Filmer, Robert, 4
Flathman, Richard, 94, 97
Frankfurt, Harry, 104
Friedman, David, 109–10, 114

Gans, Chaim, 26, 89, 98, 104
Gaus, Gerald, 29
Gauthier, David, 31
Gheaus, Anca, 53
Gilbert, Margaret, 59, 64
Goodin, Robert E., 52, 98
Green, Leslie, 103
Greenawalt, Kent, 28, 85, 89–90
Greene, Amanda, 35

Habermas, Jürgen, 78
Haidt, Jonathan, 61
Hardimon, Michael, 51–2, 59–60

Hare, Richard M., 98
Hart, H. L. A., 7, 84–5, 88, 94
Hayek, Friedrich A., 112
Hershovitz, Scott, 46
Himma, Kenneth E., 44, 46, 94
Hobbes, Thomas, 17, 22–4, 80, 109
Hohfeld, Wesley N., 8, 12–13
Horton, John, 20, 26, 28–30, 55–6, 59–60, 64, 70, 88, 91, 98, 104
Huemer, Michael, 27, 29–30, 63, 77, 90, 98, 109, 113
Hume, David, 27, 97
Hurd, Heidi M., 44

Jeske, Diane, 60

Kant, Immanuel, 32, 69, 76
Kavka, Gregory S., 24, 29–30, 89
Keller, Simon, 53
Kelsen, Hans, 7
Klosko, George, 26, 28, 35, 81, 84–6, 89–93, 98, 101, 111
Knowles, Dudley, 28, 81
Kolodny, Niko, 78
Koltonski, Daniel, 32
Kramer, Matthew, 102
Kropotkin, Peter, 109

Ladenson, Robert, 100
Lazar, Seth, 59
Lefkowitz, David, 79
legitimacy
  defined, 5, 100–1
  democratic, 46, 78–9
  as including a claim-right against interference, 100–1
  as the justifiable exercise of political power, 101
  legitimate vs. de facto authority, 4–6, 11–12, 62–3

legitimacy (*cont.*)
  as the liberty-right to enact and enforce laws, 79–80, 100–1
  as non-holistic political authority, 103
  and philosophical anarchism, 106–8
  weak notion of, 9, 79–80, 100–3, 106–8
Locke, John, 4, 17, 20–1, 23, 25, 98

Macdonald, Margaret, 55
Marmor, Andrei, 78
Mason, Andrew, 53, 59, 73, 91, 98
Mayflower Compact, 21
McMahon, Christopher, 18
McPherson, Thomas, 55
Milgram, Stanley, 63
Miller, David, 53, 112
Mokrosinska, Dorota, 73
Molinari, Gustave de, 109
Morris, Christopher, 100, 111
Murphy, Mark, 64

Nagel, Thomas, 101
natural duty
  -based theory of political authority, 30, 32–3, 67–81, 88, 99–100
  defined, 67–8
  and democracy, 75–9
  of justice, 68–75, 77–8, 99
  and the liberty-right to enact and enforce laws, 68–9, 79–80
  vs. obligation, 13, 67–8
  and the particularity objection, 70–73, 78, 80–1
  and political obligation, 68, 70, 80–1
  and the power to impose duties, 73–5, 78, 81
  samaritan, 79–81
Nozick, Robert, 84–5, 89, 107, 111–12

obligation, *see* political obligation
Ostrom, Elinor, 111

Pateman, Carole, 28
Perry, Stephen, 9, 46
Peter, Fabienne, 78
Pitkin, Hanna, 29
Plamenatz, John, 28
Plato, 17, 83, 98
political authority
  and autonomy, 44, 62, 104
  and citizenship, 6–9, 27, 49, 59–60, 65, 70–3, 78, 81, 91, 98, 100, 103
  without the claim-right to be obeyed, 9–10, 12, 100
  community-based theory of, 50–65, 68, 70–1, 73, 91, 97, 99–100
  consent theory of, 17–36, 39, 45, 48, 57–8, 60, 64–5, 70–1, 79, 83, 86, 91, 94, 97–100, 104
  consequentialist theory of, 97–8
  defined, 6–10
  and democracy, 46, 75–9
  desiderata for theories of, 14–15
  as dispersed over different persons, 14, 63
  and equality, 13–14, 18–21, 36, 63, 76–8
  the explanation condition for theories of, 15, 18, 28, 31, 33, 36, 48, 54, 63, 75, 77–8, 81, 92, 99–100

Index

fairness-based theory of, 80, 83–95, 98–100
gratitude theory of, 98
holistic nature of, 7–8, 27, 34, 49, 65, 69, 73, 88, 90, 95, 99, 103
moral limits to, 11, 19–20, 32, 43, 62, 75, 95, 107
as a moral right, 11–12, 101–3
natural duty-based theory of, 30, 32–3, 67–81, 88, 99–100
pluralist theories of, 73, 80, 90–1, 98–100
vs. political obligation, 12, 54–5, 93–5
the power to impose duties as the core of, 9–10
as the right to rule, 8–12
service conception of, 37–49, 54, 97, 99
and slavery, 105–6
the success condition for theories of, 15, 21, 28, 49, 65, 69, 88, 99–100
the target condition for theories of, 15, 19, 38, 57, 69, 92
and territory, 6–9, 26–8, 34, 49, 65, 71–3, 81, 91, 100, 103
political legitimacy, *see* legitimacy
political obligation
and community, 54–5, 59, 65
and consent, 26, 34, 36
defined, 12
and disobedience, 34, 101, 106–7
and fairness, 80, 87–8, 90–1, 93–5
and natural duties, 68, 70, 80–1
to obey the law, 12, 26, 34, 55, 68, 80–1, 87–8, 94, 101–2, 106
to pay taxes, 12, 34, 55, 68, 70, 81, 87–8, 91
pluralist theories of, 98–9
vs. political authority, 12, 54–5, 93–5
to serve in the military, 12, 34, 68, 70, 87–8
power to impose duties
and the claim-right to be obeyed, 9–10, 12, 95, 106
and community, 55, 63–5
of companies and NGOs, 30–1, 46–8, 68, 75, 98
and content-independent reasons, 11, 41, 75, 94, 106
as the core of political authority, 9–10
defined, 9–10
as essential for the state, 9, 101–3
and explicit consent, 18, 22, 28
and fairness, 93–5
and hypothetical consent, 30–1
and leadership, 32, 74–5, 78
moral and legal, 11–12, 94, 102–3, 105–6
and natural duties, 73–5, 78, 81
and normative consent, 32
of parents, 53
and the service conception, 46–8
vs. side-effect powers, 10–11, 40–1, 74–5, 93–4
Proudhon, Pierre-Joseph, 109

Quong, Jonathan, 46, 70, 72–5, 78

Railton, Peter, 52
Rawls, John, 31, 68, 71, 73, 77, 84–5, 88, 101
Raz, Joseph, 2, 10, 12, 37–8, 40–8, 64, 74, 101–3
Renzo, Massimo, 64, 81, 89
rights
 liberal, 67, 72, 76–7, 105–6, 112
 to rule, 8–11, 13–15, 18, 24–5, 28–9, 36, 49, 63, 78, 92
 types of, 8–9, 11–12
Rinderle, Peter, 71, 87, 91
Rothbard, Murray, 109
Rousseau, Jean-Jacques, 17, 62, 76

Sartorius, Rolf, 74, 98, 100
Scanlon, Thomas, 31
Scheffler, Samuel, 53
Schmelzle, Cord, 9, 46, 73
Schmidtz, David, 111
Seglow, Jonathan, 51, 53, 59
Senor, Thomas, 105
service conception
 of (political) authority, 37–49, 54, 97, 99
 defined, 37
 and the dependence thesis, 38–41, 45
 and duties, 41, 43–4, 46–8
 and the independence condition, 48
 and the normal justification thesis, 45–8, 74
 and the power to impose duties, 46–8
 and the pre-emption thesis, 42–5
Sherman, James, 41, 43
Simmons, A. John, 22, 26, 28, 34, 58, 60, 62, 70–2, 74, 81, 84–6, 88–91, 98, 103–4, 106–8

Singer, Peter, 28
Smith, M. B. E., 28, 100, 103
Soper, Philip, 98
Sreenivasan, Gopal, 32
Stark, Cynthia, 101
state, the
 defined, 6–8
 and governments, 6
 institutional roles in, 6–7, 14, 63
 and justice, 67–78, 99, 105–6, 109, 114
 and justifiable taxation, 107–8
 and the monopoly on the use of force, 7–8, 35, 112
 and national defense, 34, 85–92, 95, 113
 and non-excludable goods, 90–2, 99, 105, 111
 and peace, security, and law and order, 24, 35, 59, 80–1, 87–92, 99, 105, 109–14
 the power to impose duties as essential for, 9, 101–3
 and the state of nature, 20, 23, 69, 79–81, 109
Steinberger, Peter, 28
Stilz, Anna, 52, 78
Stockholm syndrome, 63

Tamir, Yael, 55, 57, 59
Tosi, Justin, 94–5
Tussman, Joseph, 36

van der Vossen, Bas, 57, 59, 65
Vernon, Richard, 58
Viehoff, Daniel, 39, 46, 77–8

Waldron, Jeremy, 29, 46, 72, 76
Walker, A. D. M., 98
Wall, Steven, 77

Walzer, Michael, 36
Weale, Albert, 29
Weber, Max, 7
Wellman, Christopher H., 52, 60, 62, 79–81, 98, 100, 105, 112
Wendt, Fabian, 64, 74, 98, 105
Williams, Bernard, 101

Windeknecht, Ryan G., 60, 64, 108
Wolff, Jonathan, 84, 89–90, 98
Wolff, Robert P., 44, 103–4

Zagzebski, Linda T., 46
Zhu, Jiafeng, 100, 102